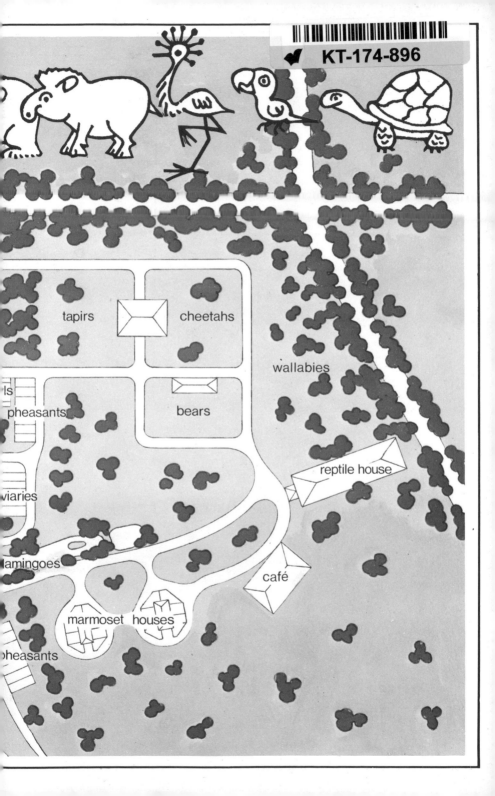

KT-174-896

The Stationary Ark

THE
STATIONARY
ARK

Gerald Durrell

COLLINS
St James's Place, London
1976

William Collins Sons & Co Ltd
London · Glasgow · Sydney · Auckland
Toronto · Johannesburg

First published 1976
© Gerald Durrell 1976
ISBN 0 00 216742 5
Set in Linotype Baskerville
Made and printed in Great Britain by
William Collins Sons & Co Ltd, Glasgow

Contents

*The drawings on pages 48–9, 86–7,
148–9, and 157 are by William Oliver.*

Illustrations

Introduction

'Be fruitful and multiply and replenish the earth and subdue it and have dominion over the fish of the sea and over the fowl of the air and over every living thing that moveth upon the earth.'

GENESIS : 28

'And I brought you into a plentiful country, to eat the fruit thereof and the goodness thereof; but when ye entered, ye defiled my land, and made mine heritage an abomination.'

JEREMIAH I :6

This is a book about zoos in general, and one zoo in particular – the one I started on the Island of Jersey.

It may be that those intimately connected with zoos may think I have been too forthright. This is because I am anxious for zoos to go on and prosper and do better and more valuable work, not dwindle and become extinct because of their own inertia and public criticism. In many aspects that I have dealt with in this book, I have, in fact, erred on the side of leniency.

However, to those who think I have been too harsh, let me issue an open invitation to come to Jersey and criticize what we are doing. We thrive on criticism and (we hope) learn from it.

Finally, may I say this? I have attempted to deal with what I consider to be a serious subject seriously, but I have tried to leaven the loaf with anecdotes that illustrate my points and, at the same time, show the amusing side of my work. If anyone objects to what may seem, on the surface, a frivolous attitude, I can only point out that if I did not find the antics of myself and my fellow animals – from politicians to peacocks – irresistibly comic, I would not have the heart to do what I am doing. The present world situation, biologically speaking, is so serious, and the future looks so dark, that one needs the fireflies of humour to light one's way.

Chapter One

'All examples included in this book are presented with the same basic reasoning : when man continues to destroy nature, he saws off the very branch on which he sits since the rational protection of nature is at the same time the protection of mankind.'

VINZENZ ZISWILER – *Extinct and Vanishing Animals*

'The fundamental limitation of our western technological culture is that it now possesses the means to cause wholesale destruction of life over vast areas in very short periods of time, but does not have an understanding of the multifarious side effects.'

DR S. R. EYRE – *Conservation and Productivity*

'Zoo biology is still a very young science and today many zoos are still run without the faintest idea that it exists. In some places no thought is given as to what the present role of a zoo either is or should be.'

HEINI HEDIGER – *Man and Animal in the Zoo*

'He that condemneth small things shall fall by little and little.'

APOCRYPHA – *The Wisdom of Solomon*

The Launching

One way and another, I have been associated with zoos throughout my life. I was smitten by what can only be called 'zoomania' at the very early age of two, when my family inhabited a town somewhere in the centre of India, a town which boasted a zoo of sorts. Twice a day, when asked by my long-suffering ayah where I wanted to go for my walk, I would drag her round the rows of odoriferous cages with their moth-eaten exhibits. Any attempt on her part to change this ritual, and my screams of rage could be heard as far south as Bombay and as far north as the Nepalese border. In view of this, it was not altogether surprising to learn from my mother that the first word that I could enunciate with any clarity was 'zoo'.

I have been saying it ever since in alternating tones of delight and despair.

Naturally, this early experience created in me a desire to have my own zoo. So, from the age of two to six, I practised assiduously for the day when I would have my own collection by assembling everything, from minnows to woodlice, which inhabited my bedroom and my person in ever-increasing quantities. At this point we moved to Greece, where I lived a life of great freedom and could indulge my passion for keeping and studying wild animals. Everything, from eagle owls to scorpions, was grist to my mill. Later, returning to England, I realized that if I was ever to acquire a zoo of my own, I would need some experience in dealing with larger animals such as lions, buffalos and giraffe, which could not – in spite of my enthusiasm – be conveniently housed in the back garden, my bedroom, nor, indeed, about my person. At this point I applied for, and was lucky enough to get, a job at Whipsnade Zoo, the Zoological Society of London's country estate in Bedfordshire. I was a student keeper, which grandiose title meant that I was an odd-job boy, who was shoved on to any section that needed a helping hand with the dirty work. In many ways it was ideal training, for it taught me (if nothing else) that, for the most part, animal work is hard, dirty and very unglamorous, but it gave me contact with a host of lovely creatures, from emus to elephants. On leaving Whipsnade, I spent the next ten years animal collecting : financing and leading ten major expeditions to various parts of the world to acquire animals for zoological gardens.

It was while I was at Whipsnade and during my first four expeditions that I began to have doubts about zoos. Not doubts about the necessity for having them, for I believed (and still believe) that zoos are very important institutions. My doubts were about the way that some zoos were run and the way that the majority of them were orientated. Until I had gone to Whipsnade, zoo-maniac that I was, I felt that to criticize any zoo, however lightly, was asking to be struck down by a bolt of lightning straight from heaven. But my experiences at Whipsnade and later, in collecting animals for zoos (thus visiting a great many of them), gave me an ever-growing sense of disquiet. As my experience grew, I came to the conclusion that there was a great deal to be criticized in the average zoo and, indeed, a lot that *needed* to be criticized if zoos, as the valuable institutions that I felt them to be, were to progress out of the stagnant state into which the greater majority appeared to have fallen, or from which they had never succeeded in emerging since their inception. However, it is simplicity itself to criticize a tightrope walker if you have never been aloft yourself and so I became even more determined to start my own zoo.

The low ebb to which zoos had allowed themselves to fall in public estimation was made apparent by the reactions I got when people found out what I intended to do. If I had informed them that I was going to start a plastic bottle factory, a pop group, a strip club or something else of such obvious benefit to mankind, they would doubtless have been deeply sympathetic. But a *zoo*? A place where you reluctantly took the children to ride on an elephant and get sick on ice cream? A place where animals were imprisoned? Surely I could not be serious? Why a zoo, of all things, they asked?

To a certain extent I understood and even sympathized with their views. Theirs was a difficult question to answer, for their conception of a zoo and mine were totally different. The core of the problem lay in the fact that in the past – and even today – few people, scientists or laymen, properly appreciate the value of a good zoological garden. As scientific institutions, they are simply not taken seriously and there is too little recognition of the fact that they can provide the opportunity for an enormous amount of valuable work in research, conservation and education. To a large extent, this ignorance has been promoted by the zoos themselves, for far too many of them seem totally unaware of their own potentialities, scientifically speaking, and continue to encourage everyone to look upon them as mere places of amusement. It is therefore not altogether surprising that both the public and the scientific fraternity regard zoos as places of entertainment, something less mobile and transitory than a circus but of much the same level of scientific importance. Zoos have, in the main, encouraged this, for to be considered scientific is, to most people, synonymous with being dull and this is not box-office.

A zoological garden can offer facilities that no other similar institution can emulate. At its best, it should be a complex laboratory, educational establishment and conservation unit. Our biological knowledge of even some of the commonest animals is embarrassingly slight and it is here that zoos can be of inestimable value in amassing information. That this can only help the ultimate conservation of an animal in the wild state is obvious, for you cannot begin to talk about conservation of a species unless you have some knowledge of how it functions. A well-run zoological garden should provide you with the facilities for just such work.

While it is obviously more desirable to study animals in the wild state, there are many aspects of animal biology which can be more easily studied in zoos and, indeed, there are certain aspects that can only be studied conveniently when the animal is in a controlled environment, such as a zoo. For example, it is almost impossible to work out accurate gestation periods for animals in the wild or follow the day-to-day growth and development of the young and so on. All this can be studied in a zoo. Therefore zoological gardens – properly run zoological gardens – are enormous reservoirs of valuable data, if the animals in them are studied properly and the results recorded accurately.

Educationally, too, zoos have a most important role to play. Now that we have invented the megalopolis, we are spawning a new generation, reared without benefit of dog, cat, goldfish or budgerigar, in the upright coffins of the high-rise flats; a generation that will believe that milk comes from a bottle, without benefit of grass or cow or the intricate process between the two. This generation or its future offspring might have only the zoo to show them that creatures, other than their own kind, are trying to inhabit the earth as well.

Finally, zoos can be of immense importance in the field of conservation. Firstly, they should endeavour to breed as many of the animals in their care as possible, thus lessening the drain upon wild stocks. More important still, they can build up viable breeding groups of those species whose numbers in the wild state have dropped to an alarmingly low level. Many zoos have, and are, doing this successfully.

Out of the thousand or so species of animal that are currently in danger of extinction, a great number have populations that have dropped so low in terms of individual specimens that it is imperative a controlled breeding programme should be set up for them, as well as the more conventional methods of protection. Over the years, people I have talked to (including zoo directors) seem to have only the vaguest idea as to the scope and importance of controlled breeding as a conservation tool and little idea of the necessity for it. In recent years, however, more progressive zoos and the more realistic

Iron bars do not only make a cage; as Surabaja the baby orangutan
demonstrates, they are also excellent for gnawing or for swinging on.

An African Civet; 'I originally brought back a specimen of this handsome grey and black spotted species from the Cameroons in 1965'.

A Saddleback Tamarin.

conservationists have been talking in terms of zoo banks for certain species. Let us call them low-ebb species. This means that when the numbers of a creature drop to a certain level, all efforts should be made to maintain it in the wild state but, as a precautionary measure, a viable breeding group should be set up in a zoo, or, better still, a breeding centre created specially for the purpose. Thus, whatever happens in the wilds, your species is safe. Moreover, should it become extinct in the wild, you still have a breeding nucleus and from this you can, at some future date, try to reintroduce it into safe areas of its previous range.

This sort of captive breeding has already helped – and in some cases saved – such species as the Père David deer, the European bison, the bontebok, the Nene goose and so on, but the zoos undertaking this work were in the minority and the help was given to only a handful of species. The list of animals that needed this sort of assistance for survival was increasing with alarming rapidity. It was apparent to me that unless more attention was paid to this particular form of conservation, a whole host of species was in danger of vanishing.

I felt that this most urgent work was one that the zoos already in existence should be concentrating on to a much greater degree than they were. Any new zoo that came into being should have it as its major objective. What was wanted, in fact, was not more large, comprehensive zoos, but smaller specialist ones, which could concentrate their efforts and devote the time and the trouble to the controlled breeding of species in urgent need of this type of help. Such a place would, moreover, be able to help some of the more obscure and un-attractive animals, which generally tended to get neglected because they were not box-office; it would concentrate on building up and maintaining (at least until they were numeric-ally out of danger) viable breeding *groups* of threatened species, and the whole organization would act not only as a sanctuary, but a research station and, most important, as a training ground. Keeping and breeding animals, particularly rare and delicate animals, is an art that has to be taught and learnt. Unfortunately, in the past (and in many zoos this is still the case) the people employed to look after the animals would be far better employing their miniscule talents elsewhere.

While the urgent need for the sort of place I wished to create seemed patently obvious to me, one had still, in those days (and to a lesser extent today) considerable opposition from what one could describe as hard-core conservationists. It was difficult to get them to see that controlled breeding was a desirable and necessary second line of defence to the conventional method of conservation, such as the creation of reserves, parks and so on. For many years, if you mentioned the subject in any august body of conservationists, they tended to look at you as if you had confessed to the belief that necrophilia was an ideal form of population control.

So ingrained was the idea that zoos were nothing more than Victorian menageries that it was almost impossible to get anyone to believe that a zoo could have a purpose more serious. The basic argument was that all zoos were badly run and few, if any, had shown any ability or desire to assist in conservation by controlled breeding programmes. Rather, by their cavalier attitude of 'there's plenty more where that came from', zoos had been a drain on wild stocks, depleting animal populations to replace the ones in their collections, lost through bad luck or carelessness, or both. There were too many zoos (so the conservationists argued) paying vociferous lip service to conservation, without doing anything worthwhile; too many zoos who only thought of a rare animal in terms of gate money and publicity and not of its importance from a conservation point of view; too many zoos whose much publicized 'conservation efforts' bore about as much resemblance to intelligent conservation work as a window-box does to a reafforestation programme.

It is unfortunate that these criticisms, to a large extent, were, and still are, valid. My plea that what was wanted now was not more normal zoos, but specialist ones, with carefully worked out conservation breeding programmes, fell on deaf ears. In this atmosphere, it required a certain amount of resolve to start yet another zoo, even if one intended that it should grow into something quite different from most of the others already in existence. I felt, however, that it was useless waiting for the approbation of the conservationists. The only thing to do was to start a specialist zoo of my own and see if it worked.

I was not in such a euphoric state that I failed to realize one important fact. Even if I succeeded, what I would have created would only be a cog in the whole complicated machinery of conservation. It would be, however, a missing cog and, I believed, a very important one. After all, however small, even cogs are important. Look how many of those minute but delicious shrimps, the plankton, were needed to build up and sustain the body of a Blue whale.

I soon found that to have flamboyant schemes was excellent, but that they would remain miasmic, without a solid foundation. That foundation was hard cash. My problem was that I wanted to create something that could not, and would not, show a profit. It was essential, if the idea were to succeed, that every penny that accrued should be ploughed back into the venture. To the average accountant – a breed of men not noted for careless frivolity – the idea of borrowing money to start something that was not profit-making, made them show every symptom of a nervous decline. The idea, when expounded to bank managers, had an even more detrimental effect. I had never realized, until then, how sceptical a really well-indoctrinated bank manager can look.

However, through the gloom came one ray of hope. I was assured that, if I could find the security, the bank would consider a loan. They warned me, in the nicest possible way, that it was their considered opinion that I would be better advised to go home, get into a hot bath and slice open a large vein. At least, that was the gist of what they said. I took no notice. The chief problem was what to use as security. This did not turn out to be quite such a problem as it might have appeared, since I had only one thing that could, loosely speaking, be called collateral and that was my authorship. This was a fragile piece of collateral if ever there was one, but I had written three very successful books and, in my innocence, there did not seem to be any reason why I should not write more. Why not borrow on these, as yet unconceived, masterpieces? Cheered by the discovery of a business acumen I had never realized I possessed, I hurried off to see my then publisher, Rupert Hart-Davis, and spoke to him long, eloquently and a trifle incoherently of my plans. So forcefully did I plead my case that poor Rupert, bemused, said he would stand guarantor for £25,000, if I took out a life-insurance policy for that amount (just in case I got eaten by a lion before I could repay the loan). This I was luckily able to do.

Now I had the wherewithal, the next problem was where to set the whole thing up. Ideally, it would be a scientific research and breeding station, not open to the public, but I knew this to be impossible. We needed the visitors to provide us not only with the running expenses, but also the cash to repay the loan and the interest. The zoo, therefore, would have to be sited either within easy reach of a large population, or else in a place that had a large influx of holidaymakers.

My first thought was of Bournemouth, which seemed ideal from every point of view. I have written elsewhere of my struggle to start my scheme there and later in the adjacent borough of Poole. I will not repeat the sorry story here. Suffice it to say that I met with such stubbornness and myopic indifference from both councils, that I abandoned all attempts to start on the south coast of England. The whole of England, it seemed, was beset with narrow-minded local councils, enmeshed in red tape and bureaucratic controls of such Machiavellian intricacy that one found oneself bound hand and foot, as though one had walked into a giant spider's web. England seemed to offer no hope, so I turned my eyes farther afield. What I really wanted, I decided, was a place which was small and made its own rules. This was not such a wild idea as it sounds, for two places immediately sprang to mind, both (in a loose sense) connected with the United Kingdom, but both self-governing. One was the Isle of Man, in the Irish Sea, and the other was the Channel Islands, lying in the English Channel, closer to France than to England. After investigation, I discarded the Isle of Man, since, lying so far north, I felt the climate would be inimical to what I wanted to do. Jersey, the largest of the Channel Islands, sounded much better. There was, however, one snag: I knew not a soul on the island.

Once again, I turned to my long suffering publisher, Rupert, and again he came to my rescue. He gave me an introduction to one Major Fraser, who lived on the island and who, unsuspectingly, agreed to show me round and help me try to locate a property suitable for my needs. So Jacquie, my wife, and I flew to Jersey and were met by Major Fraser, who drove us around the island and showed us various sites, all of which, for one reason or another, proved to be unsuitable. Feeling rather dispirited, we made our way to the Major's house for lunch. This house was Les Augres Manor, built of the warm, autumn-coloured local granite, with a large walled garden, a courtyard guarded by two beautiful fifteenth-century archways and the whole thing standing in some thirty-five acres of gently undulating farmland. I took one look at it and knew that this was what I wanted. However, I found it difficult (while breaking bread with someone) actually to evict them from their ancestral home. Eventually, I broached the subject with all the tact I could muster. To my astonishment I discovered that the Major wanted to move to England, as he found the upkeep of Les Augres too much as a private residence. He would therefore be happy to rent me the Manor, with an option to purchase at a later date, when we were more firmly established. We went down to see the appropriate authorities, who showed real enthusiasm for my idea. So, within three days, I had found the property I wanted, had obtained all the necessary permits to start and had the blessing of the States of Jersey, as the Government is called. Within three days, I had accomplished what I had not been able to achieve in over a year of fighting with a fumbling bureaucracy in England. There was a lot to be said, I decided, for being small, compact and self-governing.

In the initial stages, the zoo was a fairly makeshift affair. The animal accommodation, though adequate, left a lot to be desired in the way of appearance, but this was due to restricted funds and we hoped that it would soon be replaced, as we grew and prospered. While the zoo was coming into being, I still had to make my living and also to try to earn enough money to repay the loan. In order to get the material to write about, I had to go on more expeditions, of course, but this was a good thing from my point of view, because, for the first time, I knew exactly what was going to happen to my animals (in terms of treatment and caging) when I brought them back. Having to go on these expeditions, however, also meant that, in its early embryonic stages, I had to leave the zoo to be guided and developed by a manager. I quickly learnt that this was a disastrous mistake. Coming back from one expedition, I found that I had to cancel my plans for the next one and take over the zoo myself, to avoid the whole thing sliding into bankruptcy. The next two years were, to say the least, exhausting, for not only did I have to guard against infant mortality in the zoo by borrowing still more money, but I had to continue to write to earn my living, to try to pay back the now unpleasantly large debt.

It was fortunate that we had managed to acquire a group of hard-working and dedicated staff in our early days, for, without them, my scheme would undoubtedly have foundered at that point. I explained the financial predicament to them and pointed out that we did not know from one moment to the next if we should survive and that they would be far better off if they left and went to a place where they could obtain a decent wage and some sort of future security. To their eternal credit, they all decided to stay and so, after many trials and tribulations, after many black moments when we literally did not know if we should survive to the end of the week, we managed to pull the zoo back on course. Slowly at first, then with increasing momentum, it started to grow and prosper. So for three years we worked hard at laying down foundations on which we could build.

The place was now secure. On its gate receipts alone it could have gone on for years being nothing more than a simple, small zoo, but this was not what I had in mind when I had founded it. There were quite enough of these 'backyard' type zoos around, fulfilling no useful function. If the zoo were to expand and grow into what I had planned, then it would need financial resources from outside. The only way to achieve that was to turn it into a scientific Trust.

Later on I learnt that, in America, the word Trust is generally used to denote an organization for the distribution of money, such as a Trust Fund. In England, however, it can also mean a sort of club or association and, in such a case, it is almost always trying to obtain money rather than to distribute it. The type of Trust I wanted to create had to be a scientific one and be classified as a non-profit-making charity, so that the Trust itself would not be subject to income tax, and would have the additional benefit of being able to accept Deeds of Covenant from its supporters, thus allowing the Trust to claim the tax paid by the donors.

The original rules and regulations of the Trust were worked out by a bevy of incomprehensible lawyers and accountants. We decided to call it the Jersey Wildlife Preservation Trust. When they finally emerged, the objects of the Trust were as follows :

(1) To promote interest in wildlife conservation throughout the world.

(2) To build up under controlled conditions breeding colonies of various species of animals which were threatened with extinction in the wild state.

(3) To organize special expeditions to rescue seriously threatened species.

(4) By studying the biology of those species, to amass and correlate data which would help towards protecting those endangered animals in the wild state.

The initial membership of the Trust was built up in a rather curious way. Naturally, ever since I had first started writing, I had had in the back of my mind the idea of founding the zoo and then turning it into a Trust, so, over the years, any appreciative letters I received had been carefully filed away. I felt that anyone who enjoyed my books and who took the trouble to write to me about them would, in all probability, be willing to join the newly formed Trust as founder members. So, when the Trust was formed and launched, I wrote personally to these people and asked them if they would be willing to support us. To our delight, the majority of them did. In this way, we formed the nucleus of the Trust's membership.

There was, however, one final problem to solve before the Trust could take over and that was the matter of the original debt, incurred in founding what was now to be the Trust's headquarters. It was obvious to me that if such a Trust were to come into being and to stand any chance of growing into an organization of scientific importance, it could not be faced with a debt of some thirty-five thousand pounds as a christening present and still be expected to go on and prosper. There was only one thing to be done; I took over the debt personally. This meant that when the legal formalities were complete and the Trust came into being, I handed over the zoo and the contents, unencumbered by debt, to the first Trustees and Council.

Since that day, twelve years ago, the Trust has developed into a lusty infant. I say infant, because we still have a long way to go, but we have nevertheless laid down some very solid foundations on which to build. During this twelve years, we have done a number of things. The original animal collection, which was an ordinary, mixed zoo collection, has, to a large extent, been replaced by viable breeding *colonies* of endangered species, so that the collection now has more specimens of fewer species, which is as it should be. Over the years, our breeding record (for our size) has been commendable, with a number of species being bred for the first time in captivity (which shows we are mastering new techniques) and, more important still, a great number of rare and endangered species being bred. Our scientific record system has grown into something of great importance and from it our Annual Report (which goes to all members) has evolved as a most valuable scientific document. Our collection of animals, at the Trust's headquarters at Les Augres Manor, has now been seen by well over two million visitors and our Trust membership grows with each passing year; and with each passing year we grow in scientific and financial strength.

Just recently, I went to America to found the Wildlife Preservation Trust International, a sister organization which will allow us to expand the scope of our work in conservation. Already, this organization is not only assisting us in Jersey, but, most important of all, allowing us to expand our operations around the world. The Jersey Trust, together with its American sister organization, has done significant work in various parts of the world. We have given advice and financial help to projects such as the breeding of the newly rediscovered Pygmy hog and the various endangered species of Lesser Antillean parrot and we have led rescue expeditions to places like Sierra Leone and Mexico to collect breeding colonies of such endangered species as the Volcano rabbit and so on.

In Jersey, of course, we are still just known as 'The Zoo'. This is as it should be, but we are a zoo with a difference. We are a zoo with very clear objectives, with clear ideas of what a zoo's role should be in conservation and scientific research. In this respect, we are still a unique organization, one developing all its time, money and energies to the cause of captive breeding for conservation. We do not merely preach this type of conservation, we practise it. In this book I will try to show you where we have succeeded, where we have failed and what we hope to achieve in the years ahead.

Chapter Two

'Only the following basic statement need be repeated here : the ideal solution for a zoo is not to provide an exact imitation of the natural habitat, but rather to transpose the natural conditions in the wild, bearing in mind biological principles, into the artificial ones of the zoo.'

HEINI HEDIGER – *Man and Animal in the Zoo*

'Small rooms or dwellings set the mind in the right path; large ones cause it to go astray.'

LEONARDO DA VINCI

'One of the most frequent misconceptions which is constantly met in the zoo is the business of regarding the animals as prisoners. This is as false and old-fashioned as if in these days everybody still thought that radio and television sets contained little men who talked, sang and danced inside the sets.'

HEINI HEDIGER – *Man and Animal in the Zoo*

'Many a New Yorker spends a lifetime within the confines of an area smaller than a country village. Let him walk two blocks from his corner and he is in a strange land and will feel uneasy till he gets back.'

E. B. WHITE

The Gilded Cage

Anyone who has had anything to do with zoos must admit, albeit reluctantly, that there is precious little art in zoo architecture. The average architect in a zoo behaves like a child with its first box of bricks and will, if left to himself, produce buildings that are about as much use as they would be if they had been designed by a mentally retarded infant of five.

The main problem with zoo architecture in the past, and to a large degree in the present, is that the cages and enclosures are designed by people for *people*. It may seem odd to stress it, but when designing anything in an animal collection, there are four things which should be considered, in this order of importance :

(a) The needs of the animal,
(b) the needs of the person looking after the animal,
(c) the public who wish to see the animal and,
(d) the aesthetic aims of the architect and of the gardener who has to tend it.

Looking around the average zoo, you will find, far too often, that this order of importance has been reversed. Thus you get an edifice which may be an architectural dream and wonderful from the public's point of view, but useless for both the animal and the staff. It is, if I may be permitted to coin a phrase, what I call 'anthropomorphic architecture' and the reason it comes into being is twofold.

Firstly, the architect *does* know what he and the public want, which is something that is large and pretty (a building that salves their conscience about the imagined rigours of captivity) but he does *not* know what the animal wants and as there seems to be, generally, a complete lack of liaison between the architect and the person responsible for the animal's welfare, these architectural monsters are born.

Now it would be as foolish to expect every zoo architect to have a zoological training, as it would be to expect honesty in every politician, but it does help if the architect knows the difference between a giraffe and a dormouse, in the same way as it helps if a politician knows right from wrong. In most cases it would appear (judging by the end product) that the architect is given a brief and then goes ahead and produces what he thinks is architecturally best, with little or no consideration for the animal or the staff. There are far too many modern zoo cages which are anything but ideal for the animals within them, yet, curiously enough, it is seldom these cages which are criticized by the public, as long as they are nice and clean. Because of this attitude, many zoos have been forced to build bigger and bigger cages for animals, which, in a great many cases, only use a fifth of the space provided and would probably feel much more secure in a smaller area.

I remember visiting a brand new elephant house with a very distinguished continental zoo director who believed that, when an architect was designing something in a zoo, the animal was the customer and its wishes and needs were of paramount importance. We stood for some considerable time in silence, gazing at this monstrous new edifice, and then my friend broke the silence, speaking in a hushed whisper.

'What is she for?' he enquired.

'Elephants,' I said succinctly.

'Elephants?' he said, his eyes widening in shocked amazement, 'elephants? But why is she shaped like this, why all these pointed bits on top, what they do?'

'The whole building, according to the architect, is supposed to represent a group of elephants at a water hole,' I said. My friend closed his eyes in anguish and muttered a particularly all-embracing curse on architects, in one of the lesser known Serbo-Croat dialects. The only word that emerged clearly was architect and this was expectorated with a venom that would have done credit to a Spitting cobra.

We went inside. It was rather like going into a deformed cathedral. My friend gazed at the comparatively small area left for the animals and at the enormously distorted maze which was allowed for the public, then he let his gaze wander up to where, high above, would have hung the bells, if this *had* been a cathedral. He shuddered and again called upon the assistance of some Serbo-Croat deity.

'What for the roof so high?' he asked me, an anyway tenuous grasp of the English tongue disintegrating under the shock of such architecture. 'What for the roof so high, uh? They think sometimes maybe the elephant is meaning to fly up at night and be roosting?'

Look around at the zoos of the world and you will find them filled with such architectural abortions. Unfortunately, they are still being ripped, untimely, from the architectural womb. The whole approach to the building of cages, enclosures and houses in zoos has been wrong for years and, to a large extent, still is. There are some zoos which have made major breakthroughs, but sadly, these cases are all too rare. In zoo design today, the first question that is asked is not what does the animal need, but what does the public want? In a well-run collection of animals, you should provide the following:

1. A cage which constitutes a territory seeming suitable to the animal and providing an area of security to which he can retreat when under stress.
2. A mate, or mates, considered suitable by the animal.
3. An adequate diet, which is considered interesting by the animal and nutritional by you.
4. As much freedom from boredom as possible, i.e. plenty of 'furniture' in the cages and, if possible, a neighbour or two to have exciting, acrimonious, but unsanguinary battles and disputes with.

But, because of the public's anthropomorphic attitude, we still get these terrible animal houses, the modern equivalent to the Hindu monkey temples, so beloved of the zoos in the nineteen hundreds and in which so many unfortunate and ungrateful Rhesus monkeys shivered their way to death.

The public's concern for captive animals is laudable, but,

for the most part, misguided. They scarcely ever, in fact, complain about the things in zoos that they should complain about, but they get vociferously hysterical about the things that do not matter a damn to the animal.

People say that it is wrong to cage animals; it is wrong to imprison them; it is wrong to deprive them of their freedom. They seldom, if ever, criticize the cage; it is only the idea of the cage that they are against. The discovery that different animals have territories of different sorts and sizes, ranging from a few square feet to a few square miles, depending on the species, in the same way that human beings have back gardens, estates, counties and countries, is a comparatively new one, and we still have an enormous amount to learn about it. But it is this fact which must be borne in mind at all times when designing a cage or an enclosure for an animal. You are not necessarily depriving him of his liberty for territory is a form of natural cage and the word 'liberty' does not have the same connotation for an animal as it does for a chest-beating liberal *homo sapiens,* who can afford the luxury of abstract ideas. What you are, in fact, doing is much more important; you are taking away his *territory,* so you must take great care to provide him with an adequate substitute, or you will have a bored, sick or dead animal on your hands.

The thing that turns a cage into a territory may be something quite slight, but it need not be the size. It might be the shape of the cage, the number of branches or the lack of them, the absence or presence of a pond, a patch of sand, a chunk of log, which could make all the difference. Such a detail, trivial to the uninformed visitor, can help the animal consider this area his territory, rather than simply a place where he ekes out his existence. As I say, it is not necessarily the size which is of prime importance. This is where the people who criticize zoos go wrong, for they generally have little idea of what circumscribed lives most animals lead. The monotony of the daily round of a great many wild animals would make the average Streatham bank-clerk's everyday existence seem like the first five volumes of *The Hundred and One Nights.* The minuscule area in which some animals spend their entire lives is something which is not generally understood. In many cases, animals live, mate and die in an area that is relatively tiny, only moving outside it if some important ingredient is missing.

On the edge of a camp-site which I had in the West African rain forests there grew three trees, heavily covered with epiphytes and lianas. These trees, each about thirty feet high, standing cheek by jowl, represented the whole known world to a medium-sized pair of squirrels. In this tiny area they had everything they wanted. They had fruit and shoots and insects to eat, they had water supplies in the shape of small pools of dew and rain, which had collected where the branches joined the main trunks of the trees. Lastly, not to be overlooked, they had each other. I occupied that camp-site for four months. The squirrels were very much in evidence, from first dawn till sunset, and at no time did I see them leave the three trees, except to chase off intruders of their own species.

The three essentials that these little rodents had were the same three as most probably govern the lives of all animals, the desire to reproduce their kind and the need for food and for water. Out of these things spring the claim to territory, and territory is a form of natural cage. I am not attempting to say that the critics of captive animals are wrong to criticize, I am merely saying that they are criticizing for the wrong reasons. It is the anthropomorphic approach that is so deadly.

Going on an animal-collecting expedition teaches you a lot about territory and also about the flight distance of animals. The flight distance is a term used to describe the distance that an animal allows between himself and an enemy before taking flight. Though it varies, all animals have this, even man. If you don't believe me, try going into a field with a bull and find out your flight distance for yourself. When you have got a newly-caught wild animal, the most formidable task facing you is to persuade it to cut down its flight distance (you are the enemy, don't forget, and in constant close contact with it).

31

You also have to provide it with a new territory.

Take, for example, a squirrel. Put a newly-caught squirrel in a simple wooden box (which is what most travelling crates are) with a wire front and you will have an animal that leaps and scrabbles in terror every time you go near him. This will go on for months, perhaps for ever, for the simple reason that he is being deprived, at one stroke, of his flight distance and his territory. He cannot get away from your monstrous hand when it enters his Lilliputian world to clean and feed him.

Now put the same squirrel in the same box, but with a bedroom at one end, reached by a small hole just big enough to allow him to enter. Immediately the whole picture changes. He now has a secure area to which he can retreat when you invade his territory. From the calm of his bedroom, he can watch you clean out his cage and put in and take out his fruit and water pots, if not with equanimity then at least without too much alarm. It is important, of course, to leave the bedroom area as inviolate as possible to begin with, thus building up the animal's confidence. This is sometimes easier said than done, for some animals, like humans, are terrible hoarders and will carefully pile up in their bedroom that food which their stomachs cannot accommodate but which they feel sure will come in useful one day. When the scent of rotting leftovers becomes too all-pervading, you are forced to invade the bedroom area and clean it out, but the longer you can delay doing this, the better.

Once the animal is fully established, he will even come to look forward to your periodic invasion of his bedroom, for it means a fresh supply of banana leaves or grass, bringing with them tiny insects and seeds to be eaten, smells from the outside world to be snuffed and mused upon and then all the feverish excitement and activity that bed-making involves.

I have found that this bedroom technique works excellently with most small mammals. I have had a wild squirrel settle down so well that, after three days, when I was forced to clean out his bedroom, he actually came into it and started to tear at the banana leaves and make his bed while I was

still pushing them in. In the case of an extremely pugnacious and vociferous Pygmy mongoose, he was not only convinced, within a couple of hours, that his bedroom should be inviolate, but that his whole cage area should be as well. He accepted instantly that the cage was his territory and defended it with the ferocity of a wounded tiger. It took endless and exhausting subterfuges to get him to one end of the cage so that I could put his food and water in at the other, without risking a severed artery.

The size of the average travelling crate is governed by the fact that it is safer to transport animals in small, rather than large, cages, for, should the cages be moved by unskilled labour (which, unfortunately, they frequently are) and carelessly handled or dropped in consequence, the animal stands much less chance of being injured. However, in spite of its modest dimensions, you will generally find that an animal, having occupied a cage for some months, gains so strong a feeling of security from it that, in many cases, on arrival at the zoo it refuses to leave the travelling crate for more spacious quarters. The travelling box has successfully become its territory and the boundaries it knows and feels safe in, where it is assured of food and water.

The new cage, be it fifty times as big, does not, at first glance, offer these things. It merely holds out the promise of that thing about which human beings get so excited, greater freedom. But this is the last thing that the animal wants; he wants security and this he has already in his small travelling crate. In many cases, the crate has to be left inside the more spacious zoo cage for several days, sometimes for weeks, until the conservative and cautious creature decides to include the large cage in his territory. Even when he has accepted the larger cage, should he feel frightened he will make a bee-line for the smaller one, for it is there that he feels at home.

When collecting in West Africa once, we were brought some Demidoff's bushbabies. They were brought in by a hunter, at the very last moment, as we were moving down country to catch our ship and although I purchased them, I had

nothing to keep them in except a rather ancient native wickerwork fish-trap, measuring some two feet long by six inches in diameter. Fortunately, the Demidoff's bushbaby is the smallest of the bushbabies (being about the size of a Golden hamster that has been on a strict diet) and so these three specimens fitted very well into the fish-trap, which I had filled with dried banana leaves. The Demidoffs are one of the loveliest of the bushbabies; enchanting little creatures, with huge dark eyes, delicate ears, soft greeny-grey fur and the swift, dainty movements of thistledown blown by the wind.

When we reached the coast (only three days later) I built a proper cage for my Demidoffs and transferred them to it. Mercifully, I had not thrown away the fish-trap, for as soon as they were in their new cage the bushbabies went into a decline. They refused all food and huddled miserably in their bedroom, staring at me with great soulful eyes, like a trio of banished fairies. In desperation I returned them to the fish-trap, whereupon they revived instantly and started to feed and behave normally. On the voyage to England, the fish-trap (not having been designed for this sort of thing) started to disintegrate and had to be patched up with bits of string to prevent it from falling apart. On arrival, the Demidoffs were united in their disapproval of the zoo cage, which was approximately fifty times bigger than the fish-trap, and resisted being evicted from their wicker home with great stubbornness. The fish-trap had to be hung on the wall of the new cage and the Demidoffs lived in it for a year before venturing out into the more spacious cage. Even then, they still spent most of their time in the remains of the fish-trap and resisted all attempts to wean them on to a better-built, more spacious and hygenic basket. Eventually, after two years, the fish-trap, that had only taken the Demidoffs three days to decide was home, finally fell to pieces, but by this time the enchantingly stubborn little creatures had become used to their new quarters.

It was an animal called the Pouched rat that drew my attention to what, I suppose, could be called 'travelling

A South American Tapir with her baby.

Routine cleaning-out inside the marmoset house.

Silvery Marmosets. 'In the fragility of their metabolism one could say that marmosets were more like birds than mammals'.

territory' and, at the same time, gave me an insight into the equanimity with which some animals accept captivity. Pouched rats are large grey rodents, about the size of a half-grown cat, found in profusion in parts of West Africa. They are, for the most part, rather phlegmatic creatures, but, like all animals, they have their little quirks and foibles. One of these is what appears to be a complete absence of fear, for I have never yet met a Pouched rat who would not bite you savagely, though in an off-hand, rather absent-minded manner. The French term, *en passant*, fits the action very well.

Their other curious, but most irritating, habit (of which I was, in those days, unaware) is to collect in their giant cheek pouches any food which they cannot conveniently finish in one sitting and carry it away into their bedrooms. Thus, when I got my first Pouched rat (accompanied by my first Pouched rat bite) I was only too happy to leave his bedroom inviolate, but I immediately noticed that I was apparently not giving him enough to eat. His dish was always immaculately clean and he would peer soulfully out of his bedroom, through a web of trembling whiskers, looking like a rodent reincarnation of Oliver Twist.

Desperately, I piled more and more food into his cage, until one day I found him sitting outside his bedroom. Investigating this phenomenon, I found that his bedroom was so full of stored food that he could not get into it. I was young and inexperienced in those days and though I had mastered the technique of leaving the bedroom area inviolate, I had not yet realized that this course generally brought on a rotting food syndrome as well. Now I cut down on the Pouched rat's food and made an assault on his bedroom about once every ten days. The second time I cleaned it out, I found that, in spite of my rationing, there was a large quantity of food being stored, which meant that I was still over-feeding him. So I cut down on the perishable, soft food, like banana and paw-paw, which rotted so quickly, and increased such things as sweet potato and peanuts, which could be stored with impunity in a bedroom. That seemed to solve the problem.

Then the Pouched rat took a step which, to say the least, gave me pause for thought. I went to clean out his bedroom one evening and found it empty, except for the store of food on the banana leaf bed. In the back wall of the bedroom a neat hole had been gnawed in the wood and, to use the immortal words of my African animal boy, 'da bloody ting done go for bush'. Consoling myself for my stupidity with the well-worn saw that you learn by experience, I made a mental note to line all Pouched rats' cages with metal in future. Next morning I went to fetch the cage so that the carpenter could do just this, and there, lying curled up in his bedroom, was the Pouched rat.

At first I could not believe my eyes. It went against everything that most misguided animal lovers preach, an animal *returning* to hated captivity. It was unheard of. So I left my Pouched rat alone and observed him. Each evening, he came out of his bedroom into his cage area, ate and drank his fill and then solemnly carried what he couldn't eat into his bedroom, his cheek pouches bulging like somebody with mumps. When he had stashed it all away, he then (with much rustling and fuss) made his bed. He appeared at the hole at the back of his bedroom and sniffed the air and then went back and did a little more bed-making before reappearing and trotting off into the night. Within two and a half hours he was back. He made his way unerringly into his bedroom, had a light snack, curled up and slept peacefully for the rest of the night.

This was the pattern of his behaviour for the next two months. Then I had to move some 150 miles down country and wondered how my rat would take to this change of territory. I nailed a piece of tin over his hole for the journey, but as soon as we were established at the new camp, I removed it. The Pouched rat, with all the *sang froid* of a jet-set top executive, took the journey in his stride and, without hesitation, continued to make his bed, store his food and go for nightly walks in the forest. This continued until we got on the ship for Europe, when I had, albeit reluctantly, to line his cage with metal, since I felt that the captain of the ship,

36

light, high up in the roof. Outside, there was brilliant summer sunshine, but the interior of this cage was so gloomy that you had to peer to see the animal. In the cage there was not a single piece of furniture, no bar, no rope, no swing, no shelf. It was a glass-fronted cement box. The orang sat in the middle of the floor, carefully putting a tiny piece of sacking on its head and taking it off, over and over again. It was the only thing it had to occupy its highly intelligent and inquisitive mind. Bars, in a cage like that, would have been a blessing. When we were designing our outside ape cages, we had this and many other problems to bear in mind.

The size of our outdoor cages was dictated by the length and height of the existing building (an old granite cider-press) but within those limits, we were free to try anything. The two most important considerations were that the apes should be able to see each other without touching and that they should be able to take as much exercise as possible within the cage. The reason why apes should be allowed to see each other is the simple one of keeping them occupied. In any zoo, one of the biggest problems is the boredom of an animal and in the case of the great apes and other primates, this can become acute. Apes are highly inquisitive and long to know what is going on in the next-door cage, with a fervour similar to that of a spinster in a row of lace-curtained houses.

When you have a series of cages in a row, it is impossible to allow the inmates to see into the next-door cage without making the division with bars or wire. This would have been unsuitable from two points of view; bars or wires, we knew to our cost, allowed fingers or toes to be bitten and secondly, the stress factor created by the constant presence at his elbow of a potential rival was enough to undermine the good nature of any ape or, indeed, of any other animal. Finally, our architect came up with a brilliant arrangement. The cages were built almost diamond shaped, so that they touched but did not have a common frontier. In this way each ape could see at least a part of the cage next door and the one beyond it.

Then we had to think about the fronts. At that point in

39

our career our finances were pretty low, so we could not think in terms of armour-plated glass, which we used later on for the gorilla complex. We had to use bars, since they were the only things strong enough to keep a fully grown gorilla, orang-utan or chimpanzee confined. I did not want the straight up-and-down bars that made the Victorian menagerie such a ghastly thing to look at, so eventually, after much experiment and argument, we settled on a trellis-work, somewhat similar to those used in reinforcing concrete. Each gap was some five inches high and eight inches long, so that they were brick-like in shape. We found that these did not fuss the eye or intrude upon the visitor's view of the animal and they also provided a maximum area of climbing for the adult apes. The areas of brick-like gaps formed very elegant ladders for the baby apes when they were born. We found, indeed, that baby apes appreciate them enormously, for when they are teething there is nothing like a cold iron bar for them to chew on.

Zoos should, by now, have become much more responsible in the design of cages. Cages should be designed with great care to ensure that, from the animal's point of view, they are biologically sound; that they allow the animal to behave in as natural a way as possible yet so that it can still be easily controlled and serviced by those who look after it. In this way, each cage should become a sort of experimental laboratory, instead of being what it is at present, simply an ill-designed box for showing the animal to the public.

I am afraid that most zoo cages are biologically unsuitable for their inhabitants. This, in many cases, is not the zoo's fault, for it has to use cages which were designed and built years ago, before anyone knew as much as we do now about the animal's needs, when such things as territory, flight distance, stress factors and so on were only just being observed. But even today some fairly hideous edifices are still being constructed, mostly at colossal cost. They are virtually useless and there is no excuse for them. Antelope houses, for example, like rather inferior gentlemen's lavatories; free flight cages in

which not even a Pterodactyl would feel at home; giant exoteriums where three times the space devoted to the animal is given over to the sophisticated machinery that runs the whole thing, houses for various groups of animals where, in a desperate effort to show as many species as possible, the amount of space allotted to each creature is minimal.

I have seen some fairly terrifying things in zoos all over the world. I have seen a gibbon cage where, for many months, the only means of brachiating that the apes had was by clinging to the wire or jumping on to a series of huge concrete slabs with holes in them – a monstrosity which led one to believe that the designer of the cage was emulating (not very successfully) some of Mr Henry Moore's more obscure sculptures. The holes in these upright grey stones were also meant to provide shelter from inclement weather. I have seen elephant houses with a service passage which was too narrow to take a wheelbarrow, and it is scarcely necessary to point out that a group of elephants, charming though they are, produce enough excreta *per capita* each day to make the presence of a wheelbarrow essential. I have seen a house for small mammals with a service passage behind the cages which was eighteen inches wide, thus precluding the employment of corpulent staff and creating an interesting problem in discrimination for the unions.

I have recently seen a bird house, built at a cost which makes the mind boggle, which provides a most elegant and ingenious display. When I asked how sick birds were caught in these enormous cages, I was told that this did present a bit of a problem. The only way they had found was to shoot the bird down with a warm hose. If one had to employ such shock tactics, I would have thought one might as well have used a shotgun; the end results would have been more or less the same. This bird house was a perfect piece of anthropomorphic architecture; the very last word so far as the *display* of birds was concerned and, from the public's point of view, superb. I am not so convinced that it was equally satisfactory from the birds' point of view, yet presumably it was for them

41

that it was built.

I have seen a newly laid-out paddock for Bactrian camels, where the only thing preventing the animals from mixing with the public and biting and kicking them in the charming way that camels have, was an eighteen-inch step. I was assured that this was sufficient, as camels did not like to step down. I look forward to hearing whether the camels knew about this when they were eventually moved into their new paddock.

It is inevitable, since it is one of the cheaper forms of construction, that concrete should figure largely in zoo designs. However, it appears to be a little known fact that concrete can be disguised and it is not necessary to have every zoo building looking as if it had been designed to repel the entire Russian army. Concrete is a wholesome and useful building material in the right hands, but with this humble substance more monstrosities have been built in the zoos of the world than any other building material. I feel it must have been Lubetkin who started the rot in the 1930s with a series of zoo designs that were frightening in their uselessness and ugliness. After that, it seems, the words concrete and zoo became synonymous. In Australia, one zoo director became so enamoured of the magic material that he used it for everything. In a very short space of time, his zoo looked like one of the more overcrowded and less attractive Italian cemeteries. It was said of this man by a charming French ornithologist friend of mine : 'The problem is not so much that "X" 'as bad taste, it is that 'e 'as no taste at all.'

On the west coast of America, a city (which should have known better) handed the design of its zoo over to an architect (who should have known better). Having fallen deeply in love with cement and its sister, reinforced concrete, and having all the artistic attributes of Attila the Hun, this man has produced a zoo which is more than a shock to the system. So much concrete has been used to construct so much totally useless caging that the mind boggles. One's impulse is to clear it all away and start again, but what does one do with all that concrete? It's like being asked to eliminate the Pyramids. In

42

this zoo, I was forcibly struck by a cage which consisted of a deep cement-lined hole in the ground, with a sort of island affair (also concrete) in the middle. On top of this island was a deformed igloo made out of concrete. The whole thing looked like one of the less attractive sections of the Khyber Pass. The architect had not let his decorative instincts in any way diminish his masterly design, and one saw the concrete in its full glory, unsullied by any disguise of colour, bas-relief, incisions or modelling. I was asked to guess what this monstrous hole in the ground had been designed for and hopefully ran through a list of such things as baboons, Barbary sheep and other creatures which, being stoical by nature, might have tolerated such a precipitous and forbidding terrain. I was wrong. This monstrous, treeless, concrete bidet had been constructed, at God knows what cost, to house orang-utans, the most arboreal of the apes. Sing-Sing would have been preferable in as much as it would at least have provided barred climbing areas.

As if the poor animals and staff had not enough to contend with from the architect, we now have, sprouting up like some unpleasant fungi, what are called 'zoo consultants'. These rosy-faced cherubs, who hunt in groups, tell you that they can plan you a city zoo, providing you with everything you need, from an elephant house to a dolphinarium. It is instant zoo – just add cash. They do not, of course, claim to supply a purpose for your zoo, but then zoos are not supposed to have purposes; they are status symbols. If your city has not got a zoo, you are not keeping up with the city next door. Worse still, if your country has not got a zoo, people might think that you were only a partly emerged nation.

These curious bands are, in the main, made up of architects. They do, of course (to show their integrity), occasionally have a couple of people on the board who, without too much difficulty, can distinguish between a giraffe and a deer; possibly even a rhino and a hippo, but I wonder gloomily whether this is enough. Are these people going to be responsible for yet another rash of architectural abortions and to drive yet

another nail into the coffin of the zoos, as scientific institutions?

The whole concept of *keeping* animals is now changing and has, indeed, changed radically over the last twenty years, but zoo caging is only just catching up. Good zoos are now thinking in terms of groups of animals and not solitary specimens or pairs. More thought is going into curing that major drawback to captivity of which people so seldom think, boredom. Relieved of predator pressures, supplied with food and water and a mate, the animal has precious little left to do except to die of boredom like any other poor little rich girl. Zoos of the future should concentrate on a greater number of individual animals and fewer species. This would mean that zoos would create self-perpetuating groups of animals and thus lessen, or eliminate altogether, the necessity for a drain on the wild populations. The first step towards this is correct cage design.

Once again I must stress that what is good for you is not necessarily good for the animal, and what the animal likes is not necessarily what you like. A fair example of this rule is provided by the case of our colony of African civets. I originally brought back a fine male specimen of this handsome grey and black spotted species from the Cameroons in 1965 and we managed to obtain a mate for him from Uganda. Owing to our poverty-stricken state at that period, the den area of the Civet cage had to be constructed out of a large wooden crate that had once cosseted an aeroplane engine. This crate, when it was new, formed a very adequate den area and, in any case, we assured ourselves, it was only a temporary measure until we had funds to create better and more permanent quarters. But, as always happens when the funds became available, they had to be ear-marked for more important developments and for more important creatures. The civet dens remained untouched, except for a few minor additions and ordinary repairs.

Now, as far as we were concerned, the crate had been just adequate when new, but as it grew older and older we came to view it with loathing and walked past it with our heads

averted in embarrassment, like Church of England commissioners passing the slum property that they own. However, unlike a slum property, the inhabitants had no complaints and settled down (with the aid of some specimens I had had obtained in Sierra Leone as fresh blood) to a breeding programme which soon made us the most successful breeders of African civets in the world. To date, we have bred 49 specimens. Pairs of our home-grown civets have been sent to other zoos all over the world and from this group of animals has emerged a host of interesting material on behaviour, oestrus, copulation, longevity, number of young, gestation periods and so on. So, although the African civet is, at the time of writing, a fairly common animal and therefore not in need of a captive breeding programme, nevertheless, the experience we have had will prove invaluable should we, at some future date, find ourselves in the position of doing a rescue operation for some other member of the *Viverridae* (the Indian civet for example) or, indeed, any small carnivores, such as the interesting Madagascan ones.

We have, as I say, produced a fund of interesting material from our breeding programme of the civets. The interesting point about the operation is, however, that we have successfully bred all of them in a most unhygenic, and now elderly, aero-engine crate. We hate it, but apparently the civets love it.

Nevertheless, one has to be constantly on the look-out to see how one can improve on what one is giving the creatures. This is one of the beauties of being able to build a series of cages or enclosures specifically for one group of animals. In the old days, a monkey house would contain anything from a marmoset, the size of a rat, to a gorilla weighing 25 stone. Worse, the small mammal house would contain everything from an anteater to a rat, from an armadillo to a wallaby. Obviously, it was impossible to provide ideal accommodation for everything between these two extremes, while if one built a gorilla house and a marmoset house, one was much more likely to get nearer perfection. Of course, the habits of marmosets and tamarins, for example, vary from species to species and, indeed, from group to group and from individual to individual as well. But in building a place which is going to house *only* these tiny primates, all one has to do is to concentrate on their needs and not on the needs of a couple of hundred totally unlike species as well.

In the case of our marmoset and tamarin complex, we hope we have solved some, if not all, of the problems. Back in 1939 I had acquired a Black-pencilled marmoset as a pet and this endearing creature lived with me for eight years, at that time a longevity record for these small primates. He had been given the run of the house and garden in all weathers, the only concession to his delicacy being that there was a standard lamp in the drawing-room always kept alight, on which he could warm himself, near the bulb, in cold weather. He also had a piece of old fur coat as a bed, which was warmed by a hot-water bottle at night. Yet he thrived in these unpromising conditions and I have seen him out playing in the snow for an hour at a time, until he was driven in to his lamp to defrost his feet.

Now this was a delicate creature. In the fragility of their metabolism one could say that marmosets were more like birds than mammals. They are found in the humid and hot conditions of tropical rain forests. Yet this particular specimen happily accepted an excess of cold fresh air and what little sunlight the vagaries of the English climate permitted. He was robust in health, with a thick glossy coat. However, if I may misquote a Spanish proverb, 'one marmoset does not make a summer'. I felt he might have been a very Spartan member of his species. So in Jersey, when we had two young Red-handed tamarins with which to experiment, we gave them a heated shelter, to which they had access at all times, and a large aviary to live in. The effect was the same as it had been with my Black-pencilled marmoset. They grew and prospered, turning into a most magnificent pair of animals, whose coats were as thick as astrakhan.

In 1970, when a kind donation made possible the construction of a special marmoset and tamarin complex, this information, together with many other observations amassed over the years, was incorporated into the design. Jeremy Mallinson, our Zoological Director, has always had a deep and abiding love for the *Hapalidae,* so to him fell what he described as the nicest job he had ever been offered, the design of the new building.

Firstly, we were determined that each marmoset group should have an outdoor aviary-type cage, facing south, so that they would have the maximum exposure to fine weather. Again, we had much the same problem as with the apes, how to provide cages which would enable them to see each other, thus allowing them to bicker and feel as if they were defending a territory, and yet not to be in such close proximity as to create stress or allow fingers or tails to be bitten. The problem was solved in much the same way as it had been for the apes, by making the cages roughly shoe-box shaped, with a 'V' shaped end. This made the fronts of the cages stick out alongside each other like several 'V's; through these the animals could see each other, but without contact. By retreating into the box part of the aviary, they could have privacy from their neighbours. Inside, the whole structure was much more sophisticated and it was here that Jeremy had let his imagination have full rein.

Each of the indoor cages measured 122 cm. by 91 cm. x 152 cm. high and was custom-built of plastic (opaque self-extinguishing ICI Darvic P.V.C.), designed so that, while providing all the animal needed (sleeping box, shelf, large climbing area, infra-red lamps, etc.), it made maintenance as simple as possible. For example, the plastic floors were sloping, thus facilitating cleaning out. It is possible to trap the animals in each nest-box; this can then be removed and the animal can thus be transported to another cage with the minimum of shock. Over the years, we have kept and bred thirteen species of marmoset and tamarin and we have learnt a lot about their maintenance. We have, at the time of writing, the finest and most comprehensive zoological collection in

Europe of these fascinating and endangered little primates and hope to make our colonies larger and more comprehensive still.

In building new accommodation for animals and trying to improve on old designs, one is experimenting the whole time. Almost inevitably one makes mistakes. One tries to eliminate most of them on the drawing-board, but a few always creep in. In zoo design, one is always learning by one's mistakes and all one can do is to hope that they are minor ones. Take the use of glass as an example. This material, although expensive, is one of the best, in my opinion, to incor-

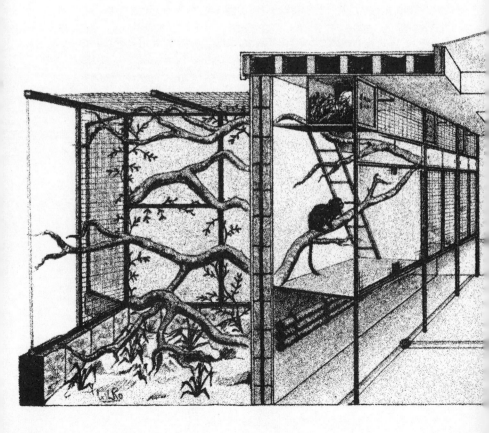

porate into animal cages. It gives a sense of spaciousness to a cage (a sense of freedom, if you like) which I feel sure is appreciated by both the animal and the visitor. You can see the animal without the visual barrier of either bars or wire. However, glass has several disadvantages, apart from the cost, and the greatest is that the animals, in moments of stress, are inclined to forget that it is there.

When we built new indoor accommodation for our South American tapirs, we let two plate-glass panels into the wall for the public to look through. Between these was the service door, the top half of which was a $\frac{3}{4}$ inch plate-glass panel

The Marmoset House

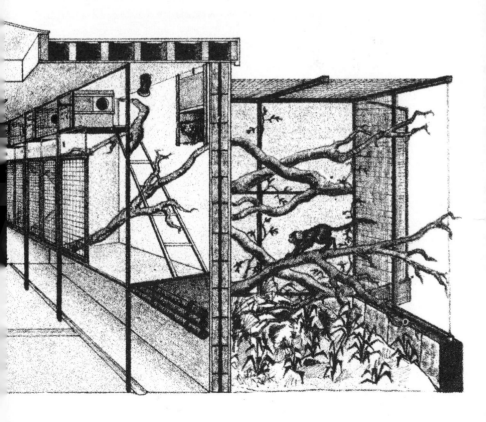

with wire fused into it. For several years the tapirs lived quite happily in this and were fully aware that the glass panels, though not visible, formed a barrier. But then one of our female tapirs, Juno, was either frightened by something (what, we cannot imagine) or had a very vivid dream that she was being pursued by a jaguar. Whatever the cause, without apparently a second's hesitation, she jumped, *not* through the spacious glass observation panel but straight through the glass and wire panel at the top of the service door. That she did not break her neck was extraordinary. That she did not die of her lacerations before she was finally caught and tranquillized half a mile away is even stranger. But the most miraculous part of the whole affair was that she was six months pregnant and, almost before her wounds had healed, had given birth successfully to a baby that was fatter and healthier than any other we had had before.

One of the other disadvantages of glass, of course, is the reaction of *homo sapiens* when in close proximity to it. Nowadays, to a certain section of the public, the sight of a pane of glass with an animal behind it is an invitation to hurl a brick. Fortunately, we have not as yet had this trouble in Jersey. We have only had gay Lotharios, determined to show their girlfriends that the diamonds in their rings were genuine by carving their initials on the glass. When this is done on a piece of specially imported armour-plated glass, costing some £600 for each six-foot by four-foot panel, you are apt to lose patience with the public and ask yourself, for the millionth time, why you bother to go to the expense of having glass so that they can get a better view of the creature on display.

One of the most complicated and expensive structures we have built to date is our gorilla complex and so far it has proved to be a great success. However, there is one minor defect. It is not big enough. Each time you start to build a cage you think it is going to be big enough and then, when you have finished it, you discover either that your animals have bred or else that, once it is actually up, it is not half as big as you thought it was going to be. But then we were not

50

to know that our gorillas, enamoured of their new quarters, were going to start breeding with a rapidity and regularity that would make the average Ford production belt green with envy.

The history of the gorilla complex is an interesting one, as it shows how luck has, to a large extent, helped us in our progress with the Trust. First we obtained our older female, N'Pongo, as a two and a half year old baby. She proved to be a charming animal in the first few days, which she spent in our guest-room because her cage was not quite ready for her. She behaved herself, in fact, better than many human guests whom we have sheltered. As she grew, of course, the urgent necessity for procuring for her a mate, or, at any rate, a companion, became very apparent, for her deeply felt (but, fortunately, short-lived) passions for various male members of the staff were embarrassing to say the least. If a twelve stone gorilla decides that she loves you and doesn't want you to leave her cage, there is very little you can do about it except comply. So in spite of our poverty-stricken condition, I purchased Nandi, another female, a little younger than N'Pongo but a fine healthy specimen. The two settled down well together; although N'Pongo adored Nandi, she made it quite clear that she was the one who dominated the cage. Several years passed and the two gorillas lived happily in their bachelor-girl menage. But it was obvious that something would have to be undertaken shortly and this presented problems that worried me.

We had to obtain a mate of the same age, or older, than our two female gorillas. Several males had appeared on the market but had been far too young and too expensive. By the time they would have attained breeding age, our two females would have been too old to breed. To procure a young adult male gorilla was an almost impossible task in itself, but we were also faced with the encouraging knowledge that, even if we succeeded, we had no guarantee that he was going to like the females or that they would like him. Nor had we any guarantee that he would know how to go about the business of breeding in the first place. So we stood a good chance of being stuck with a male gorilla whom nobody loved, as well as two frustrated spinsters. On top of this was the knowledge that the female gorillas' present accommodation was only suitable because both specimens were tame and we could go in with them; to put a semi-adult male of uncertain temperament in with them would be asking for trouble. Our finances, as always, were at a low ebb and I knew that we could not possibly find the money for a new cage. Just when it seemed that the problem was insoluble, we had two fantastic pieces of luck.

We had had some new arrivals and the local television station, Channel Television, who had always given us excellent coverage, sent up their team, as usual, to cover the event. Before we filmed the animals I was talking to the reporter, who was new. He was surprised to learn of the amount of land the Trust possessed. I pointed out, somewhat bitterly, that there was no point in having thirty-five acres of land without the money to develop it. The reporter asked if I would like to say that in the course of the interview. I told him that I had said it on numerous occasions in the past and nothing had come of it, but if he really wanted me to, I would.

We filmed the interview and that evening I watched it broadcast. No sooner had the film ended than the telephone rang. It was the operator, who apologized for troubling us, saying she knew we were an unlisted number but that she had a gentleman on the line who insisted on talking to me, as he wanted to give me some money. Never having been a snob about accepting money from strange men, I asked for him to be put on to the line. A pleasant voice informed me that it was one Brian Park talking and that he had just finished watching me on television. Was it true that I needed money? 'We always need money,' I said, feeling certain from the sound of his voice that he was good for at least fifty quid. It was then that Brian Park did the one thing that my relatives, friends and enemies had been trying, unsuccessfully, to do for years. He left me speechless, by simply saying : 'What would you do if I gave you ten thousand pounds?' It was so surprising that I could not think of a single thing to do with ten thousand pounds. By next morning, of course, I had recovered. I knew that, although we could have spent the money on a hundred different things, the new gorilla accommodation was of paramount importance. Brian, to my relief, agreed. So now we had the wherewithal for the new cage, but still no male gorilla.

It was then that we had our second stroke of luck. Ernst Lang, the director of Basle Zoo and the first man successfully to breed gorillas in captivity in Europe, had always taken a deep interest in our affairs and particularly our two un-married gorillas. Now he wrote to me and said that, should we wish it, he would sell us Jambo, a fully grown male gorilla he had bred himself. Not only that, but Jambo was a proven breeder who had sired a baby female. To obtain a fully grown captive-bred male gorilla was incredible enough; to have one that you knew was not only fertile but versed in the ways of love, bordered on the miraculous. So, almost in one fell swoop, our gorilla problem was solved. Eagerly, we set about the task of designing what we were going to call 'The Brian Park Gorilla Complex'.

Our grandiose schemes were limited to a certain extent by the site for the cage, a piece of ground sloping down to a big water-meadow. This was the sensible place for it, as it would then form a natural extension (though a separate entity) to the existing ape accommodation. However, the steepness of the slope presented several problems which we eventually managed to overcome.

The final design we were quite pleased with and so far it has worked very well. It consists of three inter-communicating dens with underfloor heating, all of which lead out through sliding doors to an area 15 m. by 10 m., containing climbing areas and a bathing pool. The novelty of this area is that it has no roof. It has twelve foot high walls, recessed at intervals, like a series of pleats on a skirt and in each of these is set a pane of glass, six feet by four. The interior of the walls is completely smooth, affording no toe or hand hold, and the windows are one and a half inch thick glass and plastic rolled together into a sandwich-like substance that could hardly be broken by a bulldozer. The whole edifice faces due south, so, having no roof, it gives the apes maximum exposure to both sunny and rainy weather, though an overhanging roof on the den area provides a verandah for them. We have recently added the refinement of closed circuit television (situated in the roof above the dens) so a twenty-four-hour watch can be kept on the apes if necessary.

In a structure such as this, it was really the detail that was the important part. The floor of the shelves had to be sloped at just the right angle to make them easy to hose down, without the gorillas feeling that they were living on the slopes of Mount Everest. The walls dividing the den area had to be barred and removable, so that the whole place could, if necessary, be made into one large bedroom. There were two reasons why barred divisions were essential. First, it meant that the animals, though separated, could still see each other and second, should we wish to use the dart gun to anaesthetize one of them or to give them medicine without the risk of going in with them, we merely entered the adjoining den and did it through the bars.

There were walls, protruding at intervals, which formed recesses. In these the animals could retire to get away from each other, for animals can get just as bored with each other (however perfectly suited they are) as human married couples. The colour scheme for the whole building had to be carefully considered. It was large and occupied a prominent position at one end of the water-meadow, so a wrong choice would have made it as attractive and unobtrusive as a gasometer. After much argument and experimentation, we chose a sort of deep olive green for the outside walls. This had the effect of camouflaging the cage in spring and summer, the whole thing merging in with the trees. The inside we decided to paint a sort of pale butter yellow. Although it looked quite nice and the gorillas showed up well against it, the snags soon became apparent. The colour was too pale and, with the cage facing due south, the surface acted like a reflector or mirror in the sunlight. The resulting glow was intense. We have now changed it to a pale blue with a sandy-coloured floor and the result is much more satisfactory, though still not perfect.

Our present major project is a new reptile breeding complex. This will be by far the most complicated building we have so far undertaken. Reptiles, by and large, receive little sympathy and so have been somewhat neglected in zoological and conservation circles. I had always thought that, while we might get kind people to give us money for accommodating mammals or birds, we would never receive a donation towards our reptile breeding programme. Then, as in the case of our gorilla problem, we had a fantastic piece of luck. We were holding, in Jersey, the first world conference on the breeding of endangered species, and among the many hundreds of people who attended were a Dr and Mrs Gaherty from Canada, who had been members of the Trust for many years. During the course of the conference, they came up to me and congratulated me on the general layout of our grounds and the condition of our animals. 'But,' continued Geoffrey Gaherty, 'there is only one thing that spoils it. You see, my wife and I are keen herpetologists and we keep and breed a lot of reptiles ourselves. Whilst the condition of your reptile specimens is excellent, we think that your reptile house is, to say the least, not good.' I confessed that I was acutely aware of the shortcomings of our reptile house (a large converted garage) and added boastfully if rather facetiously that, if Dr Gaherty could run some money to earth, I would gladly build him the best reptile house in the world. At this point I had to go and chair a session of the conference and so I did not see the Gahertys again until just before they left.

'Tell me,' said Geoffrey Gaherty, 'were you serious in what you said? If I find you the money, you'll build the best reptile house in the world?'

'Sure,' I said, 'it's only lack of funds that prevents us. Why?'

55

'Well,' said Dr Gaherty, 'among my other qualifications I happen to be an eccentric millionaire.'

'Come into my office,' I said, feeling rather faint. 'I have some preliminary sketches I did, against the day when I might meet someone like you.'

So came into being what, I believe, will prove to be a unique centre for the study and breeding of these fascinating and much maligned creatures, the reptiles. To begin with, we have no desire to have one of those awful zoo reptile houses with a host of dissimilar species kept in a constant day and night temperature throughout the year. We are concentrating on a limited number of snakes, lizards, tortoises and terrapins and all of them will be endangered species. After three years in the design stage, we are just, at the time of writing, preparing to put the final touches to the building. As usual, we are wondering what awful mistakes we have made on the drawing-board.

The unusualness of the design lies in the fact that more space is devoted to the off-view breeding area of the house than the public display, instead of the other way round as in most existing reptile houses. This is because our job is to breed the reptiles first and to show them secondly. In many cases, it is difficult, if not impossible, to attempt to breed reptiles in conventional reptile house cages, since one does not have the necessary control of the environment. In our breeding area we will have specially designed cages in which minute fluctuations of humidity, light and temperature can be controlled and a daily and seasonal rhythm can be built up. In this way we hope that, when it is the monsoon season for creatures in Borneo, we can, in miniature, reproduce the same effects. With mammals and birds, of course, they can be acclimatized and you can see tropical animals happily playing in the snow, but the metabolism of reptiles does not allow them this broad-minded attitude. They can tolerate certain minor fluctuations of temperature, but to keep and breed them successfully you have to take greater care over their climate than in the case of other creatures.

56

The whole problem of zoo design is fascinating, and one that is still in its infancy. It is not an impossible task to marry good public display with excellent living quarters for the animal, but it is done in too few zoos and, where public display is the stronger motivating force, the animal always loses out. I would think that a regime of stringent economy is not a bad one for zoo directors and architects. A structure need not cost thousands of pounds to be effective, as we have proved over and over again. The refinements are nice to have, of course, but it's surprising what you can do with humble sums of money and materials. It is, after all, only the humans who worry about the expensive part of the cage design; the aesthetic side. The animals only want a place that feels right as a home, and if you give them this, you get your rewards.

Chapter Three

'They were followed by a platter on which lay the most enormous wild boar. On its head was perched a cap of a freed slave; on his tusks hung down two baskets lined with palm leaves, one was filled with Syrian dates, the other with Theban dates. Little sucking-pigs, made of pastry and baked in the oven, surrounded the animal as if they were pressing on the teats . . . Drawing his hunting knife, a slave gave the wild boar a great stab in the belly and suddenly, from the opening in the animal's side, flew out thrushes.'

P E T R O N I U S – *Trimalchio's Feast*

'The Greeks named this bird Upupa because it lines its nest with human dung. The filthy creature feeds on stinking excrement. He lives on this in graves . . . If anybody smears himself with the blood of this bird on his way to bed, he will have nightmares about suffocating devils.'

T . H . W H I T E – *The Book of Beasts*

'A Spider is an air worm, as it is provided with nourishment from the air, which a long thread catches down to its small body.'

T . H . W H I T E – *The Book of Beasts*

The Complicated Commissariat

It was that brilliant gourmet, Brillat-Savarin, who said, 'Tell me what you eat and I will tell you what you are'. This simple rule unfortunately cannot be applied to animals. Neither can the reverse, because simply knowing what an animal is merely puts it into a very rough gastronomic category, which takes no account of its personal likes or dislikes, or indeed of our ignorance of its diet in the wild state. Thus you will get an animal, classified by the textbooks as 'strictly vegetarian', which has a tremendous hankering for fish or meat, and a 'strictly carnivorous' animal who will behave with drooling idiocy at the sight of a bunch of grapes.

Until comparatively recently the whole question of diets in zoos had received scant attention and, to a large extent, it seems that its importance was not recognized. Anything unfit for human consumption must be ideal for animals, was the general line of thinking and still is today in far too many zoos. But the animal in the wild state, unless it be a carrion feeder from choice, gets the freshest of everything, and it was this simple fact that was not appreciated. I have seen in far too many zoos (some of them zoos of repute) stale meat and fish being fed to animals and with them rotting vegetables and over-ripe and mildewy fruit. This, put at its most mercenary, has always struck me as being a false economy. If you are a farmer and you starve your animals or give them inferior food, you do not expect to get a good milk yield or to breed stock successfully. Why, then, does a zoo director expect to get strong and healthy animals and good breeding results by feeding inferior food? To what extent in the past animals have been labelled 'difficult' simply because they have been wrongly fed, would provide an interesting, if depressing, line of investigation for zoo historians.

Coupled with zoo diets (which were, in many cases, more

harmful than helpful) there was once again, the baleful influence of the zoo-going public. Going to the zoo to 'feed the animals' became the accepted thing, accepted, unfortunately, not only by the public, but by the zoos themselves. Feeding by the public, directly or indirectly, helped the exchequer. The fact that what the public fed was generally the wrong sort of food and in too great a quantity, resulting in sickness or actual death, was accepted by some zoo authorities as a fact of life. I know from bitter experience how difficult it is to prevent people from feeding in zoos, but in those days no attempts whatever were made to stop them; rather it was encouraged. There were a few rather feeble attempts made to get people – if they had to feed the animals – to feed them the right things, but by and large this was a failure. The public preferred to feed the deadly peanut, the chocolate bar and the ice-cream (all purchased in the zoo shop) and the animals, gorging themselves like children on these delicacies, died of impacted bowels, enteritis, or thrombosis as a result.

Today, in all the more advanced zoos, feeding by the public is forbidden, and quite rightly too. But it is one thing to forbid and quite another to prevent. The average member of the public seems to think that he has an unassailable right in any zoo to do three things without let or hindrance : to scatter litter around him like dandruff; to prod animals with umbrellas and sticks or to throw stones at them in order to stir them up if they are so ill-mannered as to be asleep or stationary; and to feed anything in sight that will accept what he has to offer, be it peanut or sugar-lump, lipstick or razor-blade. These latter items are not exaggerations. We have had them both fed to our animals, together with aspirins, bits of broken bottles, sheets of plastic and, once, a filled and lighted pipe. The public, on the whole, appears to have even less knowledge of what is dietarily desirable for wild animals than many zoo directors.

It is a curious fact that animals which are extremely conservative about new foods as a rule will, when they get to a zoo, with unerring accuracy go mad for the one food that will either do them the least good or the most harm. If they displayed this trait in their character when they were newly caught, it would make the animal collector's lot a much easier one, for he would then have something to tempt them with. The lack of this can try his patience severely, for long before the animal arrives at the zoo the collector has the unenviable task of teaching it to accept a new diet. This is a task as fraught with difficulty and disillusionment as trying to inculcate the elements of French cuisine into the average English boarding house.

At the extreme end of the scale, there are the animals who are monophagous. These demand a monotony of diet so extreme that even a medieval saint would feel that it was carrying the mortification of the flesh too far. Pangolins or Scaley anteaters, for example, hailing from Africa and Asia, exist happily on a strict diet of ants, in some cases the black, indigestible-looking tree ants, who reek of formic acid to the extent that your eyes water when cutting up a nest.

In the clear forest streams of West and Central Africa lives a remarkable creature that rejoices in the name *Potomagale velox,* or giant Water shrew. This black insectivore – the only representative of its kind, though it has a distant relative in Madagascar – is about two feet long, with a dark mole-like fur and minute eyes, no collar-bones, a swollen muzzle, so that its head looks like the head of a hammer beforested with whiskers, and a tail that is flattened from side to side like a tadpole's. It is nocturnal, aquatic and (at least in the Cameroons, where I caught it) lives exclusively on a diet of chocolate-coloured fresh-water crabs. It seemed to me when I caught my first *Potomagale velox* and examined it that anything so strong and otter-like, a creature adapted, apparently, to the pursuit of a wide variety of prey, could not possibly exist on such a restricted diet. Even the most fanatical crustacean addict would, I felt, occasionally want to have a chance of fresh fish or frog, or even a water snake steak. So I experimented and tried my Potomagale on large beetles, delicious fish in many shapes, sizes and colours, obese frogs, water snakes of varying lengths and baby birds and eggs. It was all to no avail. The Potomagale viewed with disdain these suggested additions to his diet and stuck to the scrunchy fresh-water crab. This, as far as I could see, contained practically no nutriment, since it was composed almost entirely of carapace.

My problem was, of course, twofold : first, I could not take a large enough supply of fresh-water crabs on the ship with me (my Potomagale was consuming some thirty-five crabs per night) and, second, no European zoo could provide such an esoteric diet. There is, alas, no zoological Fortnum & Mason where such gastronomic rarities can be purchased. Therefore this creature of limited taste had to be taught to eat something different. This was easier said than done and required the employment of a certain low cunning.

I obtained from the local market a large quantity of dried fresh-water shrimps, used to add piquancy to curries, ground-nut chops and other African foods. These shrimps, powdered up, I mixed with minced meat and raw egg. The Potomagale, at feeding time, was voracious and this, I hoped, might give me my opportunity. I killed a number of crabs and stuffed them full of my shrimp and meat mixture; then I gave him an ordinary, undoctored crab which he devoured in a few quick scrunches. Having thus lulled his suspicions, I threw him a stuffed crab. He was half way through it before he realized that there was anything wrong with it. He spat it out to examine it through a web of quivering whiskers, then, to my delight, he finished it off. Over a period of weeks, I managed to get him to the stage where he was eating my special mixture from a dish, with a scattering of chopped-up crab on top, just for the look of the thing.

Another problem child is the Giant anteater, the largest of the group. With its long, icicle-shaped head, its pennant-like tail and its huge, bear-like claws for breaking up the rock-hard termites' nests that provide its food, it is a spectacular animal. It was in the highlands of Guyana that I captured my first one, pursuing him on horseback, lassoing him, avoiding his slashing claws while we bundled him, hissing like a gas-main, into a sack and transported him back to camp. Once there, I tethered him to a tree and put my mind to the task of teaching him a new diet. I knew that the diet worked out for Giant anteaters in the past had been raw egg, mince-meat and milk. The tricky business of persuading the anteater to take this unlikely substitute in place of its beloved termites was the crucial problem and one that was glossed over in the few manuals on zoo-craft that existed.

Sometimes animals are so hide-bound in their prejudices that they won't try a new food; indeed, in many cases, won't even approach closely enough to smell it. That this is pure prejudice I have proved by the fact that, at some later date, the animal will consume, with pleasure, the food that it had rejected with such horror when it was first offered. In some cases, the suspect food even becomes its favourite.

My anteater was not quite as narrow-minded as that, but he did regard the first bowl of milk, with raw egg and meat floating in it, as being as suspect as a light snack run up by one of the less attractive members of the Borgia family. Then I had an idea. I broke open a termites' nest and obtained a handful of the large, but singularly unattractive-looking in-habitants. These I scattered on a large green leaf, which I then floated on the surface of the milk. The anteater, per-ceiving his favourite food, unfurled his foot-long, sticky tongue and began to browse on the ants. Naturally, his probing tongue kept flipping under the leaf and within a few minutes he was lapping at the mixture as though he'd never eaten anything else in his life or wanted to. At the next meal, I did not even have to camouflage the food with termites. He licked the bowl clean, juggling the last fragments of meat into his tube-like mouth with his tongue in the most elegant fashion.

Stubborn though newly-captured animals can be, there generally comes a point when they surprise you by doing a complete volte-face. When I went out to Sierra Leone one of my aims was to obtain a group of the Black and White Colobus monkeys. These handsome creatures are primarily leaf

63

eaters and so the job was to get them to eat a different sort of leaf to the one that they were used to. Actually, the job was threefold; first we had to teach them to eat the local types of greens we could get in the market, then to eat the food we would give them on the voyage home and, finally, to eat what we could provide them with when we got to Jersey. With this in view, I put in cold-storage on the ship that we were going to travel back on, crates of lettuce, cabbage, carrots, spinach and other delicacies that I thought might tempt the Colobus. All this was arranged, of course, long before I even got to Sierra Leone and before we knew we were going to catch any Colobus, let alone get them down to the coast. However, we did finally catch seven specimens, successfully adapted them to captivity and got them to accept the various green stuffs that we could get in the local native market.

We finally got down to the coast and on to the ship and immediately the Colobus went into revolt. All of the delicacies procured and transported at colossal cost to please them, our beautiful crisp cabbages and spinach, our carrots and tomatoes, were looked upon as though they had been so much deadly nightshade. It became a major problem to keep the monkeys alive. There was only one thing to do. My secretary, Ann Peters, was detailed to do nothing else all day but make the Colobus eat, while we dealt with the rest of the collection. It became a battle of wills between the Colobus and Ann, and luckily Ann won. She managed to persuade them, by cajolery and abuse, to take just enough food to keep them alive. Once we were back in Jersey, I felt that we would have oak and elm and lime leaves to tempt them with and things would be better. The moment we arrived in Jersey, however, the Colobus, who had been ticking over on a diet only a shade above starvation level, overnight decided that all the things we had been offering them were just what they wanted and that they could not eat enough cabbage, spinach, carrot and tomatoes.

You can't lay down any hard and fast rules, for the individual animals vary so enormously. Once, on a collecting trip to the Cameroons in West Africa, I managed to catch

The Gorilla Complex, 'one of the most complicated
and expensive structures we have built to date'.

White-eared Pheasant – handsome and exceedingly rare.

The Ibis breeding ground – a cliff face built
with rough granite slabs.

three Angwantibos. These are strange little biscuit-coloured lemuroids that look something like demented arboreal Teddy-bears and, up to that time, had never been brought back alive to Europe. Only one person that I knew of had ever kept one of these little creatures alive and so information on their habits was scanty. However I did know that, as well as fruit and buds, they would take small birds; so three times a week they had plump weaver birds included in their diet. Now all three Angwantibos had been caught within a five mile radius of my camp in identical terrain and so one could be pardoned for thinking that their eating habits would not be dissimilar, but, when presented with his bird, Angwantibos number one would proceed to devour the whole thing, except for the feet and head; number two would eat only the breast of his; whilst number three would perform a skilful trepanning job on top of the skull, lick out the brains and leave the rest.

Every day, with any collection of animals, you are learning, generally with surprise, that their tastes are just as varied, their likes and dislikes as firmly implanted, as the clientele of any large hotel. We had not been established long in Jersey before we discovered that two of the most unlikely species had a passion for the humble herring that knew no bounds.

These were the South American tapirs, supposedly strictly vegetarian, and the lions, carnivores it's true but surely unlikely to get herrings in the wild state? In the case of the tapirs, it made us wonder if (since the animal is partially aquatic in the wild state), when the streams dried up into pools during the dry season, trapping the fish, the tapirs did not go fishing. But that tapirs in the wilds are followers of Isaac Walton has never, to the best of my knowledge, been recorded. The idea of fish, especially herrings, turning up with anything like regularity in any lion's wild diet is remote to say the least. The smell of raw herring must have been so ambrosial that our lions could not resist adding them to their diet.

Whatever the reason, in both cases we were grateful for this liking, for the herring is a useful and pungent vessel in which to conceal medicines, should the need arise. In meat or fruit a pill would be detected and spat out disdainfully, while lurking in the depths of a really ripe herring it is undetectable and swallowed with every evidence of satisfaction. The list of subterfuges of this kind which one has to learn seems endless. For example, spiders act as a laxative to some birds, whereas, in our apes, fresh pineapple has the same effect. One of our African civets always used to 'kill' his bananas (not other fruit, only bananas) using a method that presumably civets use in the wild state to kill their prey. He would first grab and shake the banana into what he imagined to be a state of semi-consciousness, then he would fall on it repeatedly with his shoulder until the banana was a flat squishy mess smeared over the ground. Satisfied that it was dead, he would then eat it with relish.

Of course, when animals develop a great liking for some particular thing, you have to be careful, for they will sometimes start consuming it to the exclusion of everything else. One of the great things in keeping animals is to try to prevent them growing bored of their diets. Thus one is constantly trying out new things, introducing new sights, colours and smells into the diet to relieve the monotony. A grape, for example, contains nothing more nutritious than a small proportion of sugar and a great deal of water, but nevertheless, it is of inestimable value as a tit-bit, an exciting addition to the basic diet, like a jelly at a child's party. But the danger of over-doing it, of inducing a grape-fixation, must not be ignored.

We had a Douracouli once in South America, one of the most enchanting of all the monkeys. Owl monkey is another name for it and a most descriptive one, if you can imagine a fur-covered owl. It is also curious in being the only nocturnal species of monkeys. We had not had this delightful creature long before she went off her food. There seemed no particular reason, as she was in good health, but with dull and uninterested eyes she picked at the food we gave her with the dispirited air of a guest in a hotel dining-room which boasts

66

an international cuisine. It was obvious that she needed something to stimulate her flagging appetite. My wife, by some alchemy and at enormous cost (we were in the Matto Grosso at the time) succeeded in obtaining a couple of tins of cherries, of all unlikely fruit. On their being opened, we found they bore no resemblance whatsoever to the cherry one was used to; they looked as though they were an unsuccessful line in Christmas decorations, made out of inferior velvet and of such a virulent red that they would have made even Snow White hesitate before accepting one. However, our Douracouli took one look at these violently-coloured fruits and decided that this was manna from Heaven. So addicted did she become, in fact, that she eschewed all other food and it took us an enormous amount of time and trouble, not to mention money, to wean her back on to a more nutritious, if less colourful, diet.

Once you have removed your animal from the wilds, one of the biggest problems you face is how to combat boredom. Animals spend most of their time in the wild searching for food and, once you have eliminated the necessity for the search and the stimulation of hunger, boredom can easily set in. It is like a man who, having worked for thirty-five years in an office or a factory, suddenly finds himself in retirement and faces an empty life. In many cases he dies quickly, out of sheer boredom. Animals suffer in a similar way, so you try to combat this by the introduction of new foods into the diet, even if they contain little or nothing of nutritional value, and by the careful spacing of those foods which are both favourites and of nutritional value. In the absolutely ideal collection, of course, each animal would be fed individually, so that you would know its exact food intake. In many cases, when it is necessary for the animal to be kept in groups, this is difficult or impossible. We are able to feed at least our apes and some other animals individually and we have found what an enormous help it is to be able, in case of sickness, to know exactly, down to the last teaspoonful, of what an animal's daily intake of food consists.

As I said, the animal spends a large part of its daily life searching for food. Even if the food is not forthcoming, the act of searching is of great importance. Therefore we have found that, for example, providing small mammals with rotting logs as often as possible has a very therapeutic effect. The whole process of relishing the smells of the log, the effort required to disembowel it, the hopeful search for something edible in the pile of rotting bark and wood, is of the greatest psychological help to the animal, even if it does not acquire much in the way of nourishment from its exercise. Ideally, of course, animals should be fed ten or fifteen times a day, but this would require a staff of such magnitude as to make the idea, however desirable, uneconomic. We have found, though, that with a great many creatures it is necessary to feed them twice or three times a day. To keep a group of animals occupied, however, it is not necessary to produce a three-course meal, three times a day. The scattering of a handful of corn or sunflower seed on the floor of the cage containing a group of monkeys or squirrels, for example, will provide little in the way of food, but will keep the animals occupied for ages, searching for the grains and bickering enjoyably among themselves as they do so.

As I said before, scant attention was paid to zoo diets in the past and in many zoos there is still a total lack of imagination used either in working out the diets, or in presentation. Probably the most important major breakthrough in the keeping and breeding of tropical animals came with dietary experiments and discoveries pioneered at Philadelphia Zoo under Radcliffe. His discoveries were of great importance to the keeping and breeding of wild animals.

Working with the animals at Philadelphia Zoo, Radcliffe was puzzled by the fact that, although common animals had good longevity records, they failed to breed. More delicate animals were eating well, but the mortality rate among them was high. After a lot of investigation, he discovered that while, on the surface, the diets fed looked perfectly adequate, they were lacking in a number of trace elements, minerals and vitamins. He experimented and eventually came up with a form of pellet which contained all the additives that the diets needed. These pellets were fed in addition to the normal diet and an immediate increase in successful breeding resulted, as well as a general improvement in the animals' condition and longevity. This pioneer work was later taken up by Lang and Wackernagel at Basle Zoo in Switzerland and Radcliffe's additive was extended in scope and improved on, with spectacular results, not the least being the successful breeding of gorillas for the first time in captivity in Europe.

When the result of the work at Basle was published, it had a somewhat mixed reception; it was described to me by one eminent English zoo director, for example, as 'a lot of bloody nonsense, feeding animals on nothing but pills' and by another broad-minded and go-ahead director as 'a lot of rubbish, stuffing animals up on vitamins, instead of giving them good food'. Having lived most of my life on the continent, I lack, to some degree, that insular, blinkered smugness of character that makes the English so charmingly unique. So, overlooking the fact that this whole new process had been invented by one set of foreigners (the Americans) and added to and improved by another (the Swiss), I nevertheless felt the matter was of great importance and well worth investigating. I therefore paid a visit to the fountain-head, as it were, Basle Zoo. I was vastly impressed by what I saw and what I was told by Lang and Wackernagel and I returned to Jersey determined that we would put this new dietary system into operation as soon as possible.

We had long conferences with Mr Le Marquand, the zoo's miller, for some of the ingredients could not be obtained easily and we had to find suitable substitutes. Finally we took delivery of the first cake, as we called it. There had been a lot of discussion as to whether the ingredients should be presented in the shape of a loaf, a biscuit, or in some other form and we had eventually decided to stick to the Basle Zoo method, which was a sort of dough-like cake, served in pieces about an inch long and half an inch wide. I had been warned by Lang that, if my animals were anything like his, they would fanatically resist the introduction of this new element into their diet. He said that he had had, in many cases, practically to starve his animals before they would even try the new substance Now, however, they all adored it.

Lang's prognostication proved right; our animals displayed all the symptoms of appalled horror that you would expect from a missionary to whom you had offered human flesh *en casserole*. We wondered, in the face of such stubbornness, whether perhaps our dough-like substance tasted different from Lang's; since some of the ingredients were not the same, was the first result perhaps unpalatable? Like a board meeting of Peek Frean, we stuffed our mouths full of the substance and compared notes. We found the cake to be pleasant-tasting with a nice nutty, biscuity flavour. It was, we agreed, very acceptable. However, our liking it was not much help. The animals did not find it palatable and that was that. There was only one thing we could do and that was to add something to the taste, to make it more attractive.

Most of the things we at first thought of would have been burnt out during the baking process. It was when we reached what appeared to be a dead end that I thought of aniseed, a time-honoured substance for baiting traps and for stealing dogs. We tried it and, to our delight, the aniseed flavour came through loud and clear. We decided, wiping the crumbs off our mouths, that the product was now delicious. To our great relief, the animals felt the same. Now it is a pleasure to watch one of the gorillas, on being handed a dish laden down with delicacies ranging from grapes to raw eggs, sift through the food with a thick black forefinger and carefully extract the biscuits, in order to eat them first with the rumbling, growling, avalanche-like noises that gorillas make as a sign of extreme pleasure.

In addition to the ape nuts, there was also a special carnivorous variant that we used to sprinkle over the meat and other foods given to such things as the lions and servals. This was of enormous value. In Jersey, a large proportion of the bull calves are slaughtered at birth or within a few days of it. Prior to our arrival on the island, this valuable source of protein was simply buried, as it was useless as veal, for the calves were too young and, moreover, had yellow fat, which, for some reason, makes it unsaleable. From our point of view this was a blessing, since it meant that we would have an almost unlimited supply of fresh meat, free. The advantage of being able to feed freshly killed meat of this sort, with the bones, skin and stomach as well, was, of course, enormous. However, we did find that the meat of these young calves did not contain the amount of nutriment, in the shape of vitamins and minerals, that was to be found in the meat of adult horses and cattle. The carnivorous mixture added to our meat provided those essential ingredients that were missing.

Diet and disease, of course, are inextricably bound up : feed the wrong diet, or one lacking in some vitamin or mineral, and you open the door to a host of diseases. A case in point was the killing malady, called cage paralysis, which, as it turned out, had nothing whatsoever to do with cages.

Among the new world primates in particular, and occasionally in those of the old world as well, you got a strange form of creeping paralysis for which there was no known cure. It was called cage paralysis because it was felt vaguely that it was caused by incarcerating animals in small cages where they could not get sufficient exercise. This was supposed to cause their muscles to atrophy. I had noticed however, that the disease attacked monkeys kept in quite spacious quarters, which seemed to indicate that the cause might be dietary.

When I was an animal collector, this disease was probably the most widespread and serious – since apparently incurable – among captive primates. It would start very gradually and almost imperceptibly in the hips and hind limbs of the animal. The creature would start to shuffle rather than walk, and show a disinclination to move about a lot. Gradually it would lose the use of its hind limbs and the paralysis would creep upwards to immobilize the rest of the body. Long before this stage, however, the animal would probably be destroyed since, as I say, there was no known cure. While collecting in South America, I had experienced several outbreaks of this unpleasant disease among my monkeys and on my return I discussed the matter with one of the few intelligent veterinary surgeons that I knew. Competent veterinary surgeons you can find; intelligent ones are as rare as unicorns. She suggested, stressing that it was only a guess, that the disease might be due to a lack of phosphorus in the diet. We checked the diets I had been feeding and found that they contained a full complement of phosphorus. 'Well then,' my friend suggested, 'it might be that they are unable, for some reason, to absorb the phosphorus.' She suggested injecting D3, which she said would alleviate this condition. At that precise moment, there was no monkey suffering from paralysis, so I tucked the information away in the back of my mind and forgot about it.

It was not until we came to Jersey that I had a chance to try it out. We had a Patas monkey from West Africa, one of those charming, long-limbed, ginger and black animals, who was attacked by the disease and succumbed with extraordinary rapidity. In a very short time she became totally paralysed, her entire body immobile; she could still breathe and eat and drink, but only if we held her head up. It was then that I remembered what my friend had suggested and hastened to procure some D3. There was no precedent for its administration, but as the drug was considered harmless I gave the Patas a massive dose. She was so far gone by then that it was, almost literally, kill or cure. To my astonishment, within forty-eight hours there was a marked improvement. I gave her another, slightly less massive dose. Within the week, she was moving her limbs and within a month bounding around her cage with such vigour and *joie de vivre* that it seemed impossible that she'd ever been that flaccid, immobile creature on the edge of death.

The animals that were particularly prone to this unpleasant disease were the marmosets and tamarins and they succumbed very easily, because of the fragility of their make-up. The first sign of a shuffling gait in one of these animals had been a death sentence in the past. Now, an immediate dose of D3 and the animal had no further trouble. Naturally it was necessary to inject a massive quantity compared to the size of the animal and, naturally, the marmosets and tamarins took grave exception to this. However, it was for their own good and we had to do it. Now, fortunately, we can give D3 orally, so that they get it in their food. It is pleasant to know that the so-called cage paralysis is a thing of the past, for I know of no more harrowing experience than watching an otherwise healthy animal lying with death creeping up its body, and being powerless to help it.

The importance of these additions to the normal food is indicated, I think, by the figures of our breeding results. In any collection of animals the feeding is of paramount importance if you are to obtain good breeding figures and, in our case, the breeding results are probably one of the most important, if not the most important, aspects of our work. I have tried to show that feeding animals is not as simple and as straightforward as it appears. We are still very far from knowing all the answers to the dietary requirements of animals kept under controlled conditions. This is due, in the main, to our ignorance about wild diets and their composition. We know that some creatures, at certain times of the year, visit special mineral or salt licks and feed off certain fruits, berries or fungi, but we do not know the importance of this to their overall well-being. We are only just learning that the diets that we have been giving to animals, though they may be varied enough to keep the animals alive and well, may not be sufficiently imbued with the right vitamins or mineral traces. These might make all the difference to the length of time an animal lives, its general health and well-being and its breeding potential.

Realizing what an untouched field of research lies here, we have recently, with the aid of a most generous grant from the Freund Foundation in America, set up a nutritional laboratory. Our first job is to break down all our present diets, so that we know precisely what they contain. While doing this,

73

we are going to amass as much information as possible about wild diets and their seasonal variations. Thus we will have some sort of comparison to work with and from this we hope to improve our feeding, to establish what vitamins or minerals are missing and, of vital importance, to discover the best way of including these in our diets. To this end, we are setting up an experimental nursery in which we plan to grow selected shrubs, vegetables, fruits and herbs. Obviously, if one discovers that an animal should have a certain vitamin or mineral in its diet and one can give this as a plant or fruit that the creature likes, it is a much more satisfactory way of administering it than simply by opening a bottle. Also, you can discover new herbs, shrubs, vegetables and fruits which the animals may like. These can form a useful addition even if they are of no nutritional value, for they enliven and vary the diet and, in cases of illness, can play a most important veterinary role by acting as a stimulant.

It is also necessary to learn – and we hope we shall do this eventually by field studies – at what time of the year certain things are eaten and why. Is it because the foodstuff is only available at that special time, or is it freely available all the year round, but only eaten at that particular time for some other, specific reason? The monophagus Koala bear is an example of what I mean. Its diet is restricted to two species of Eucalyptus leaf. At certain times of the year, a Koala moves from x species to y species, for the simple reason that the shoots and the young leaves of x species, when growing, contain enough prussic acid to kill.

It is vitally necessary for us to learn more about wild animal feeding habits, for the lack of one simple ingredient could mean the difference between success and failure. To say that animals in the wild state have some very curious food fads is no exaggeration. For example, it was known that marmosets and tamarins consumed live food in the shape of tree frogs, lizards, baby birds and eggs, as well as fruit and buds. Just recently, however, two other startling ingredients have been added to the menu; sap and, of all unlikely things, bats. The

74

sap is obtained by the animal making grooves in the bark of branches with its teeth and then lapping up the tree juice that oozes out. The bats are captured when they are roosting in hollow trees during the day.

If it is possible that one day we may be returning captive-bred animals to the wilds, either to populate an area where they have become extinct or as an aid to a dehabilitated species, then the diet becomes of even more vital importance. To take an extreme and slightly ludicrous, though not un-likely, example : if a species of owl, seventh generation born in captivity, had been trained to eat white mice, it might well starve to death if released in the wild and found only brown mice available. Another aspect that has to be borne in mind is that the wild foodstuffs, for the most part, are provided in considerably less generous quantities than those received by the cosseted captive animal. It may well be that, before release, it would be necessary to put the animals on a preparatory diet, rather like someone training for the Olympics. These are all problems that lie in the future but, in conservation, the future has a habit of becoming the past with frightening rapidity. That is why we are already starting on this line of research.

To economize on food is a false economy. Of course there are cuts one can make. If one finds that carrots contain more goodness than hot-house grapes, one tries to feed carrots, which are cheaper. But one must never eliminate the hot-house grape completely. It serves a purpose, if only as an aperitif or an appetite stimulant. Anyone who has spent any time in hospital would agree that the food may be well balanced, nutritious and bursting with vitamins, but it still lacks that Epicurean touch that makes the taste buds, metaphorically speaking, stand up and cheer. When you are dealing with a collection of wild animals, it is essential that at all times their taste buds should be catered for.

Chapter Four

'Weasel . . . Some say that they conceive through the ear and give birth through the mouth, while, on the other hand, others declare that they conceive by the mouth and give birth by the ear.'

T . H . W H I T E – *The Book of Beasts*

'A comprehensive literature exists on how to manage domestic animals, dealing at length with every conceivable detail. Feeding, breeding, transmission of hereditary characters, pedigree, distribution, market value, pathology, training and so on have long been the subject of basic research and have become the specialized departments of an impressive science. On the other hand, the study of how to keep wild animals in zoos can hardly boast of even the most general outlines; all it has to show is a collection of more or less disconnected pieces of advice and some facts.'

H E I N I H E D I G E R – *Man and Animal in the Zoo*

'Partridge . . . Frequent intercourse tires them out. The males fight each other for their mate, and it is believed that the conquered male submits to venery like a female. Desire torments the females so much that even if the wind blows toward them from the males they become pregnant by the smell.'

T . H . W H I T E – *The Book of Beasts*

'In his research on mountain gorillas living wild in the area of Kabara G. B. Schaller (1963) found a mortality of 40 per cent to 50 per cent during the first six years of life; the mortality is highest in the first year of life. In this connection it should be remembered that gorillas only have a few enemies apart from men.'

H E I N I H E D I G E R – *Man and Animal in the Zoo*

'Ethel and Bernard returned from their Honeymoon with a son and heir a nice fat baby called Ignatius Bernard.'

D A I S Y A S H F O R D – *The Young Visitors*

A Multitude of Matings

It may sound obvious, but the acquisition and introduction to each other of a *compatible* pair of animals is the first prerequisite for successful breeding. Many people consider that all that is necessary is for a male and female of a species to be confined in a cage together, but the whole business is infinitely more complicated than that. Marriage arrangements are sometimes of great complexity and, as the animal gets rarer, careful considerations of blood-lines take place that would do credit to a similar arrangement among royalty. You may go to endless expense and trouble to obtain a mate for something, only to find that the two animals hate each other on sight, or, what is probably worse, tolerate each other and settle down to a dull existence together without issue. If they take an instant dislike to each other, you at least know where you are, but if they settle down to be just good friends, you are in a quandary. Will this toleration grow into something deeper? Will this liaison have a happy ending? You find yourself asking these questions with all the earnestness of the editor of a woman's magazine when presented with a new serial.

Sometimes you have to face the fact that the only pair at your disposal are incompatible. Then you have to do the best you can. Our White-eared pheasants were a case in point. We acquired two pairs of this handsome and exceedingly rare pheasant via a Dutch dealer from Peking Zoo. The exact status of this species in the wild is uncertain; it has never been common and may, indeed, be extinct or seriously depleted throughout its range. These birds were the first to come out of China since 1936. At the time we received them, there were only fifteen specimens in captivity and most of these were either past breeding age or non-breeders for some reason or another. So it was of the utmost urgency that we bred from our two pairs and firmly established a breeding pool of these lovely birds.

On arrival, one of the cock birds was suspiciously tame, almost lethargic. Within twenty-four hours he was dead. The post mortem finding was aspergillosis, a fungus disease of the lungs for which there is at present no cure. This left us with one cock bird and two hens, and the cock only took a real interest in one of the hens. Naturally, as always happens, this hen got egg bound with her first egg and, in spite of all we could do, she died. This left us with only one pair of birds and an incompatible pair at that. Our chances of establishing the White-eared pheasant in captivity seemed so slim as to be non-existent.

Then came what we were convinced was the final disaster : the cock bird was frightened by something during the night, caught his leg in the wire and severely wrenched it. He could only just walk and we thought gloomily that, in such a condition, he would be unable to tread the hen, even if she displayed hitherto hidden charm for him. To our astonishment, however, he suddenly found the female attractive and, by some prodigious acrobatic feat, succeeded in treading her. From this happy experience she produced her first clutch of

78

eggs, nineteen in all, out of which we successfully reared thirteen youngsters under a foster bantam, which had undergone a course of wide spectrum antibiotic to ensure that she had no disease she could pass on to her foster babies. Gradually our numbers increased. Our first job, in order to ensure the perpetuation of the species under controlled conditions, was to establish – on loan – breeding pairs at the Washington, Antwerp and West Berlin Zoos, The Pheasant Trust and Clères Zoo. Since then, we have bred and reared a total of 112 birds and now feel we can afford to sell pairs to selected zoos and aviculturalists. The money from these sales is paid into a special account to be used for the purpose of purchasing rare creatures for the Trust's collection or to help with providing accommodation for such creatures. Thus the White-eared pheasants are now helping other species that are in a similar plight.

Marriage and the begetting of young is (among animals other than man) an infinitely complex problem. Quite apart from the personal likes and dislikes of the creatures involved, there are many other aspects to be considered. Are the animals solitary in the wild state, except for the breeding season? If so, this presents special problems. For example, with our West African civets, who are solitary except during the mating season, we have to judge when the female is in oestrus. Only when she is, do we let the male in with her. Now the male civet bites the neck of a female when mating with her, as tigers do, so it is only by the wounds on the neck of the female that we can tell that mating has been successful. We then quickly remove the male before really vicious fighting can break out between the two sexes.

When we have a perfectly compatible pair, living happily together and not breeding, we ask ourselves what we are doing wrong, for unless the animal is physically incapable for some reason, the fault lies with us, in the diet or the accommodation that we are providing. In the past, too many animals have been labelled difficult or non-breeders, as if the fault lay with the animal and not with the human who was controlling its life. At one time it was considered 'impossible' to breed such things as rhino and hippo for example, but at last the trick was found and now they are bred with comparative ease. I must explain what I mean by trick, in case it sounds too facile. I have always maintained that, allowing for the solving of the basic difficulties (food supply and accommodation for a Blue whale, for example) there is no animal species one cannot keep and breed successfully under controlled conditions, once one has discovered the trick. The trick might be anything ranging from the obvious one of finding the right mate, to providing the right area for the young to be born in, the right food, the right increase in nourishment when the female is pregnant, down to simple things such as the right number of ropes to swing on. The trick is always there; it's up to one's ingenuity to discover it and the animal generally gives one precious little help.

It is very gratifying when one finally discovers the trick, gets every detail correct and sees one's efforts crowned with instant success. It happened in the case of two very dissimilar animals with a rapidity that was quite astonishing and provided one of our big success stories. The first was the Waldrapp, or Bare-faced ibis and the second the Jamaican Hutia, a small rodent endemic to that West Indian island. Both these creatures are in danger of extinction in the wild state and so it was essential that breeding colonies should be set up in captivity.

In the case of the Waldrapp, its future in the wilds is, to say the least, grim and there seems little chance of its survival. It is a medium-sized ibis, with a long curved beak, sombre black plumage that flashes iridescent purple and green when the light strikes it, a bare reddish coloured face and a strange crest of long feathers on the back of its head, which makes it look as though it is wearing a feather wig that has slipped back, revealing its bald forehead. They are colonially-minded birds who congregate on cliff ledges to construct their nests and rear their young. At one time, they spread from the Middle East via North Africa to as far into Europe as Switzerland.

Jamaican Hutias –
'they resemble large
greeny-brown
Guinea pigs and
waddle around,
hind legs spread
widely apart, as
though they had
just wet their
pants'.

A Ring-tailed
Lemur, which
provided the first
breakthrough in the
lemur breeding
programme.

Bali, the most
sweet-natured and
stupid of
orangutans, with
her baby,
Surabaja.

Surabaja with her
playmate, Tunku.

Harassment of their nest sites (for the young were considered a culinary delicacy) and, later, poisoning of both adult and young birds by DDT and other pesticides, greatly reduced their range and numbers, so that now there are only some 500 pairs left. There are only two known nesting sites : one in North Africa, which is rapidly dwindling (presumably owing to pesticides) and whose whole future is threatened by the construction of a dam, and another, which has the misfortune to be situated right in the middle of the village of Birecek, on the Euphrates. In the old days in this town, the birds received a measure of protection, since their arrival at the nesting site was heralded by a great festival.

As the town of Birecek grew, however, and the inhabitants became more 'civilized' and 'sophisticated', the festival was dropped. The birds turned, almost overnight, from being a reason for rejoicing to being a pest – birds who were unmannerly enough to bespatter the inhabitants of Birecek when they slept on the roofs of their houses. Small boys stoned the young on their rocky nesting sites while in the local fields (where the adult ibis assisted man by eating insect larvae) the land is being smothered with a massive coating of insecticides. Although both the International Union for the Conservation of Nature and the World Wildlife Fund are attempting to get the local people to protect the birds again, the chance of this – the biggest colony of 250 pairs – surviving, seems remote. The only hope for the future of these birds seems to lie in a captive breeding programme and then, possibly, reintroduction into some parts of its former range, perhaps in Switzerland or North Africa.

In 1972 we acquired two pairs of Waldrapp from Basle Zoo. They were young birds, but as soon as they became adult, they made one unsuccessful attempt at nesting. The nest itself was not a particularly brilliant construction and the eggs that they laid turned out to be infertile. Shortly afterwards, when the full plight of this ibis in the wild became known, we decided to embark on a breeding programme; first to try to establish the bird firmly in captivity and second to aim at a reintroduction programme some time in the future. To this end, we acquired two more pairs from Tel Aviv University in 1975.

It became apparent fairly soon that the aviary in which we housed the birds was – from their point of view at any rate – in some way inadequate. We felt that in order to achieve success we must do two things : raise the height of the aviary and supply the birds with a cliff face on which to nest. Lacking funds for this project, we presented our plan to our sister organization in America and they gave us a generous grant. Our first step was to write to every zoo in the world that possessed, or had possessed, Waldrapp, to find out what breeding successes they had had and to get the designs of the aviaries in which they had kept their specimens. To a large extent, this information was unhelpful and contradictory, since no two zoos kept their Waldrapp in identical accommodation. In some instances, the birds had bred in what appeared to be unsatisfactory circumstances, while in other, apparently more attractive, surroundings, they had refused to nest. All we could do was to construct what we considered to be the best accommodation and hope that it was right for the birds.

The ibis breeding site, when completed, consisted of an aviary 40 feet by 20 by 12 feet high. It had 6 feet by 3 feet glass panels let into the wire at intervals and its back was constructed in the form of a cliff face out of rough granite slabs. At intervals, nesting sites of different sorts had been built into the cliff. Since the type of nesting site used by these birds in other zoos had varied so enormously, we felt we should supply as many different varieties as possible. In some cases we constructed natural ledges (sloping backwards towards the cliff face, so that the eggs and young would not fall off); other nest sites consisted of wooden containers (like wooden boxes, with no top and one side missing) let into the granite fascia.

When this complex was completed, with its large pond, cliff and ample flight area, it seemed to us to be ideal. The only thing that remained was to find out whether the ibis agreed. From the way they flew to and fro, landing on the cliff face and inspecting the nesting sites, mumbling to each other in their strange, guttural language, it seemed as though they approved. Then, almost before they had learnt the geography of the new cage, they started carrying nesting material up to the wooden boxes, inset into the cliff for this purpose. We watched with bated breath as two nests were built and seven eggs were laid. As these were all laid by young birds, we thought we would be lucky to hatch and rear two out of seven, so when all seven eggs hatched and when the parents successfully reared six chicks out of the seven (the seventh was a weakling that rapidly succumbed), to say that we were delighted would be to put it mildly. It meant that we had almost doubled our colony in one fell swoop and made the possibility of a reintroduction programme seem infinitely less remote.

In the case of the Jamaican Hutias, we had the same sort of good luck; success, due to finding the right formula, which, in this case again, was suitable caging. We had acquired our Hutias in a rather strange and round-about way. Every zoo director worth his salt keeps up a correspondence with a wide variety of people in remote parts of the world, in the hopes that one day they may be able to procure some rare and desirable animal for him. In my case (since people read my books and write to me in consequence) my correspondence is a widespread daisy chain, reaching from Peking to Penambuko. Among my correspondents was a Mrs Nell Bourke, who one day wrote from the lovely island of Jamaica to say that she had enjoyed my books and added – most unwisely – that she would be happy to try to procure for me any Jamaican creature that took my fancy. She made the offer in a spirit of bonhomie and I am sure that she was filled with grave misgivings when, by return of post, she received a letter from me, asking if it would be possible to obtain some Jamaican Hutias. Having made the offer, however, Nell Bourke stuck to it and, with the aid of her friend, Mary MacFarlane, set about the task of Hutia hunting.

First, of course, official blessing had to be obtained, since Hutias are one of the few remaining endemic mammals in Jamaica and, although regularly hunted and eaten when found, are strictly protected as an endangered species – an anomalous state of affairs not found in Jamaica alone, unfortunately. They then enlisted the services of a Hutia hunter, with the euphoniously alliterative if unlikely name of Ferdinand Frator. In due course, to everyone's surprise (including Ferdinand Frator's) he managed to procure three live Hutias; a mother, father and their offspring. Nell Bourke had already received a massive list of instructions from me, preparing her for this unlikely (as I thought) eventuality, together with detailed drawings of travelling boxes that looked like the plans of the Russian missile bases in Cuba and would undoubtedly have had Mrs Bourke arrested had they been found in her luggage. After much trial and tribulation, the Hutias were crated and despatched on an aircraft. Nell Bourke sent me the following telegram : 'Hutias arriving London Airport flight BEA xxx. Pray. Nell.'

To our delight, all three Hutias arrived in perfect condition, unalarmed, it appeared, by their long flight. They resembled large greeny-brown Guinea pigs and had a most endearing way of waddling around, hind legs spread widely apart, as though they had just wet their pants. On sexing them, we discovered, to our annoyance, that the baby was a male, which gave us two males to one female. Writing to Nell Bourke to tell her of their safe arrival, I pointed out that, while in no way wishing to appear as if I was looking gift Hutias in the mouth, the ratio of one female to two males was one which, to say the least, formed a somewhat risky basis for a breeding programme of any seriousness. Could she, I enquired delicately, press the valiant Mr Frator into service once more and try to procure more families? To her eternal credit, in spite of all the traumatic experiences she had undergone in obtaining the first Hutias, Nell Bourke undertook to try to get some more. To our amazement and delight she succeeded triumphantly. So, in a relatively short space of time, we had four pairs.

From our experience with the first trio, we had decided that, to undertake a serious breeding project, we needed new and improved accommodation. Once again, our sister organization in the United States provided us with a grant and with it we constructed a spacious series of glass-fronted cages in the Mammal House, each one equipped with wooden tunnels and bedrooms, furnished with large logs and lit by red light that allowed one to see the animals, while, from their point of view, they were in complete darkness. We reversed their day and night cycle. Turning lights on at night and switching them off during the day when only the red light was left burning. Within a very short time, the Hutias were sleeping peacefully during our artificial day and appearing happily during the artificial night which we had created, so that visitors could see them going about their affairs.

As in the case of the ibis, the Hutias took only a short time to show their approval of the new surroundings and within three months the first family gave birth to twins. The babies, a little bigger than a Golden hamster, were fully mobile from the moment of birth and, indeed, were observed eating solid food when only twenty-four hours old. In rapid succession, two other pairs of Hutias set their seal of approval on the new accommodation by breeding; producing twins and a set of triplets. It was enchanting to watch the three sets of parents with their offspring. The babies were full of character, rushing to and fro around their apartments, bouncing up and down like rubber balls and uttering shrill piping cries, while they played hide and seek in the straw and around the logs. They would rush up to their patient and long-suffering parents, sit up on their fat little behinds and begin to box their father's or mother's face. When the parents became bored with this, they would roll the baby over on its back and gently bite its stomach, while the infant kicked and wriggled convulsively, uttering loud giggling squeaks of pleasure. It gave us great pleasure to see the tubby babies

85

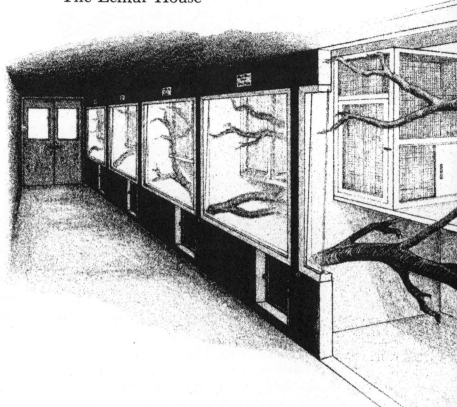

playing so exuberantly with their parents,
but it was sobering to remember that, from the day
I first wrote to Nell Bourke on the subject of Hutias, it had
taken us three years to achieve this wonderful breeding success.

Of course, on occasions, one may not be doing anything
wrong. It might well be that the species in question takes a
long time to settle down and consider its new quarters home
territory. Our collection of lemurs, six species in all, have
given us endless trouble and we are only just beginning to
feel that we are doing the right thing and progressing in the
right direction. Basically the problem lay, I feel, with the fact

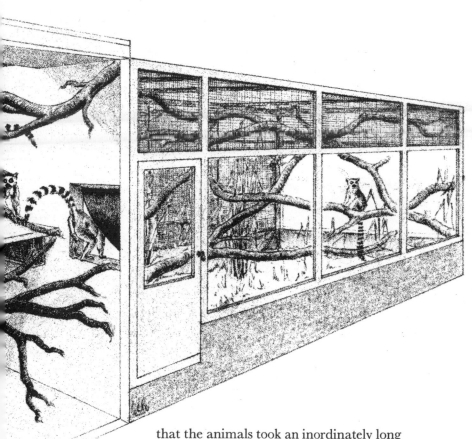

that the animals took an inordinately long
time to adjust themselves to their new surroundings.
The situation facing the Madagascan fauna generally, the
lemurs in particular, is pretty grim. Pressure of human
population, culminating as always in the thoughtless elimina-
tion of forests, both by destruction to provide farmland and
overgrazing by domestic livestock, has created a situation
where the whole of that enormous and zoologically fascinating
island (in its own way as interesting as Australia) is in grave
biological danger. Some species can cope with the threat of
man's numerical superiority, his relentless destruction of

habitat and the depredations of his domestic stock, but other species, many of them lemurs, will probably vanish within the next fifty years.

Our lemur collection had been spread, higgledy-piggledy, round the grounds and, although lively and healthy, had never shown any signs of wanting to breed. We felt that if we were going to make a serious contribution to the establishment of breeding colonies, our lemurs would have to be provided with new quarters.

Our new lemur range, when we had completed it, consisted of six units. The roofed-in area, which included a public corridor, gave the lemurs heated indoor accommodation, measuring 2.4 by 1.5 x 2.7 m. high. This led into outdoor cages, measuring 6 long by 2.4 wide by 3 m. high. The end of each bedroom and outdoor cage consisted of a large glass panel, which allowed the lemurs to have an uninterrupted view of the public and the public of the lemurs.

From the outset, the lemurs, Ruffed, Mayotte, Mongoose and Ring-tailed, approved of their new abode which gave them plenty of fresh air and sunshine. The cages face south-east and have ample space for movement. The lemurs' diet had been meticulously worked out from our own observations and experience, with additional know-how from ten other lemur collections scattered round the world. Now we felt that all we had to do was to sit back benignly and wait the flood of babies.

To our chagrin and astonishment, no babies were forth-coming. In spite of bitter experiences with a host of different species, one is always shocked and hurt when, after one has taken infinite pains to ensure the well-being of one's animals, it turns out one is not doing the right thing. Although the lemurs ate prodigiously, sang lustily both day and night and copulated with all the joyous abandon of participants in a Roman orgy, nothing came of it for some considerable time.

Our first breakthrough was with the Ring-tailed lemur. Polly, our youngest female, gave birth to a lovely male baby, but unfortunately it was dead on the floor of the cage when we found it. X-rays showed there was no air in the lungs, which proved that it had been born dead and had not died from neglect, and post mortem findings proved that there was nothing internally wrong with it. It was just one of those inexplicable things; half-expected, because we had noticed on many occasions that the first babies of most animals are more liable than not to be failures. It is almost as though a young female's body and her maternal instincts are not fully aroused at the time of the first baby and it takes one such birth to get her into training, as it were, for the future. The affair had at least proved to us that Polly was fertile and that she had some maternal instincts, for the baby had been carefully cleaned, the umbilical cord severed and the afterbirth eaten. With her second baby, the following year, she had no difficulty and successfully reared it to maturity. We hope that now she has done this once, she will have no further trouble.

Once Polly had started the ball rolling, the other lemurs followed suit. Our next birth was with the Mayotte Brown lemur, one of the rarer species. Here again, the first birth was a failure. However, we have now had three successful births. But, from the moment of completing the new lemur accommodation to the first breeding, it took three years, which goes to show the time and patience involved in trying to set up an intelligent and viable breeding programme. This is of particular relevance when one is dealing with a species that is decreasing in numbers in the wild state at a ferocious speed.

In any breeding programme, one's difficulties seem to proliferate as one progresses. Once one has the right mate and has learnt when to introduce him, if the animals are solitary, or how to stimulate him by the production of more than one wife or rival, if these are available (a more difficult problem to solve), then one gets to the point when the female in question becomes pregnant. Now comes the thorny problem – does one leave the male with the female? To do so can be a disaster, where the father commits – or his presence forces the mother to commit – infanticide, yet it can also sometimes be essential for the well-being of the offspring.

Two problems we had among our primates give some idea of the difficulties in the animal marriage market. Among the South American marmosets and tamarins a type of Women's Lib has been unobtrusively, unvulgarly and very successfully practised for some considerable time. The female, when she gives birth (almost invariably to twins), hands them over immediately to the father for cleaning and supervising. From that moment on, the male plays a large part in the rearing of the young, taking his share of carrying around the ever-increasing weight of the babies, slung on his hips like paniers on a donkey, or on his back like a furry, mis-shapen knapsack.

In order to find out just how important the fathers were in the rearing process, we did a study of the movements of twin Red-handed tamarins. The results were fascinating, showing how the physical labour of carrying the young was divided. It is a very important factor, for, as the young develop and get heavier, though they tend to move about on their own, they still return to the parents for attention and in moments of stress. In this instance, the father unexpectedly died when the young were three days old, and so the mother had to rear the two babies single-handed. This she did successfully, but towards the end, when the young were half as big as she was and still demanding to be carried on occasions, it was obviously a very exhausting and exacting process for her. However, she faced up to her task and the two babies grew into healthy adults.

It was particularly interesting that, in spite of the difficulties facing the female, this was the first time that the Red-handed tamarins had been successfully reared to maturity in captivity. It was apparent from this that, in the case of the tamarins and marmosets, the male played an extremely important role, even though the female, if determined and a good mother, could rear the young without him. It obviously followed that the father in this case must be left with the female and not separated when the young were born.

We once had a visit from an exalted member of the hierarchy of a very well-known zoo indeed who, while admiring our marmoset babies, confessed that they had had little success with this group. They had bred, but the young had died. However, he went on, obviously in total ignorance of marmoset behaviour, they hoped for better luck next time as they intended to remove the male.

The question, 'Shall we remove the male?' is one that excites, among zoo people, the same sort of controversy as was once aroused in ecclesiastical circles by the question of whether or not Adam and Eve had navels, and with much the same inconclusive results. Of course, it depends not only on the species but on the individual in question. But however well you think you know your male, and even if it is biologically valid to leave him with the young, you may still end up with dead offspring. The rarer the animal, of course, the greater the risk and the more difficult the decision becomes.

Orang-utans are probably the rarest of the great apes and are the most threatened by extinction in the wild state. It has been estimated that if the drain on the wild stocks of the Bornean orangs and the Sumatran sub-species is not rigidly controlled, this fascinating red primate will be extinct in the wild state within the next twenty years. If this prognostication is true – as, alarmingly, it seems to be – it is of vital importance that zoos should build up breeding colonies of these animals, not only to prevent the drain on wild populations, but to ensure that the species survives, if only in captivity.

We are lucky enough to have acquired both the Bornean and the Sumatran sub-species and to have successfully bred both of them. When the female Bornean, Bali, was pregnant, we had her separated from the male, Oscar, since it was the unanimous opinion that, magnificent as Oscar was and bursting with character though he might be, he was a real devil. No one wanted to predict what his reactions to a baby would be. So he lived a bachelor life while Bali was undergoing the last stages of her pregnancy. Then, finally, she gave birth to a fine healthy baby, a female called Surabaja.

Bali was of a temperament so sweet and gentle and idiotic that we were inclined to think of her as feeble-minded. It was fortunate for us that we had this view, for, although immensely proud and enamoured of the baby, she had not the faintest idea of how to deal with it. It is universally accepted now that, among the apes, the babies get their basic sex education from watching adults; thus a young male learns how to mate by watching his father and a young female learns how to look after a baby from her mother. We do it with celluloid dolls; apes do it with real babies. But if an ape is taken into captivity at a very early age, it does not have a chance of learning these techniques and this can cause great difficulties when it comes to breeding.

Bali had come to us when about two years old and so she should have had the opportunity to watch some crêche habits in the wild. Perhaps she had but had forgotten about it, for, as I say, she was sweet-natured but not overburdened with brain-power. Be that as it may, she was delighted with her daughter, cleaned her up very nicely, then clasped her firmly in her arms. And that, as far as she was concerned, was all you had to do with babies. The poor infant, now on her hip, now on her back, now draped over her head, searched desperately and unsuccessfully for a nipple with which to assuage its thirst, while Bali just sat there, beaming benignly.

Eventually we were forced to go into the cage with her and show her how to hold the baby so it could feed. This took several days, but in the end she got the hang of it and seemed enchanted with so novel an approach to baby rearing. It was unfortunate that, whilst Bali was rearing Surabaja, the male, Oscar, died, a loss which I shall deal with later. When it was time to remove Surabaja from her mother, we mixed Bali with a young male orang whom we had called Giles. Although Giles was much younger than Bali, they settled down well together and we hoped they would soon mate successfully.

Unfortunately, Giles is a really Machiavellian character and takes a delight in frustrating everything we do. When we tried to get urine samples from Bali to send to the laboratory so as to see if she was pregnant, Giles did all he could to prevent it and to considerable effect. We continued trying, of course, but were lulled into a sense of false security by the fact that Bali did not *look* pregnant. Orangs are generally fairly pot-bellied, which makes it difficult to tell, but with her first pregnancy Bali had been enormous, whereas now she looked only slightly bloated. We felt sure she was not pregnant. Then, while we were still trying to defeat Giles and get a urine sample off her, she gave birth. It was very early in the morning and, by the time the staff came on duty, Giles had stolen the baby from Bali and killed it. The only good thing to be said about this was that at least we now definitely knew that Giles would have to be removed before Bali gave birth again, but this knowledge was hard won and the incident put our whole orang breeding programme back a year.

With our Sumatran orangs, Gambar and Gina, we had a different situation. Gina was a somewhat sour and untrustworthy character while Gambar was one of the most intelligent apes I have ever had the privilege of meeting. The moment you met him and looked into his alert and observant eyes, you were aware of a powerful intellect. He had come to us on loan from the Zoological Society of London and, while he had been with them, he had actually sired a baby and remained in the cage when it was born, so we knew that he would not be murderously inclined. Nevertheless, he was such a powerful, exuberant animal (he brachiated more than all our other orangs put together) that we felt he might well unwittingly kill or damage the fragile baby during his boisterous perambulations around the cage. We had divided Gambar's and Gina's den in the same way as the gorilla dens, with a removable, barred partition. We felt that if Gambar was on one side and Gina and the offspring on the other, he would be able to see and even to touch his baby if Gina allowed it, but there would be no risk of him sitting on it by accident, while performing his circus acts round the cage.

The Sunday morning when, according to our records, Gina was about due to give birth, Philip Coffey, who is in charge

93

of our ape colony, saw her trying to make a nest out of sawdust and wandering about in a restless fashion. She was given half a bale of straw, with which she immediately constructed a nest. This done, she lay on her back in it with her legs wide apart. Very soon and with no complications, the baby, a fine male specimen, was born. Gambar, at this point, was allowed to see Gina and the baby through the bars and evinced a certain amount of interest.

After about forty-seven days, when the baby, christened Tunku, had developed and grown strong, Gina regularly played with him, holding him away from her body with her feet and hands and dangling him in the air. After this, she frequently left the baby climbing on the barred partition of the den and there Gambar would play with him, putting his hands through the bars to touch him. Gambar was at all times remarkably gentle for such a large and boisterous animal. Sometimes he would squat on the floor and push his hands through the bars. Tunku would sit in his father's cupped hands and be lifted up and down, a form of exercise which appeared to afford both father and son immense gratification. Once the baby was strong and agile enough, Gambar was reintroduced to Gina and the baby. He behaved impeccably. Tunku would, at times, climb all over his father, and Gambar, with enormous patience, would allow his hair to be pulled, every bit of his anatomy examined, fingers poked into his eye and even bits of food removed from his mouth, without complaint.

Most apes can walk upright like human beings, but only for short distances and with their legs bent at the knee. Gambar, however, could walk with his legs absolutely straight and with his feet flat on the ground; the swaggering, corpulent walk of a retired Brigadier-General on the sea front at Brighton. Moreover, he does not do this for short lengths of time but on occasions walks round and round the cage for a considerable period, with a militant look on his face as though inspecting a guard of honour. This is amusing enough to watch under any circumstances, but when Gambar walked round and round like that, carefully carrying his infant son in his huge hands, the sight was irresistibly comic.

The complexities of successful marriage among animals is shown by the difficulties we had with our gorilla group, for, in trying to establish these creatures we ran the gamut of practically everything that could happen. As I said earlier, we acquired the female, N'Pongo, when she was an estimated two and a half years old. We then obtained Nandi, another female, slightly younger. N'Pongo, from the first, was a charming extrovert, with great gaiety of disposition and firm ideas about her own importance. Though she liked Nandi from the moment of introduction, N'Pongo made it quite clear that it was *her* zoo that they were living in, the staff were *her* friends and Nandi would do well to remember it. She was too charming and good-natured an ape to develop into a sadistic bully, as many animals would have done in the circumstances, and she treated Nandi with great affection but considerable firmness. Thus, for five years the relationship was one of mutual affection and regard, with N'Pongo in many ways taking the place of the male. The relationship, in fact, was one which, in a girls' school, might have been described as unhealthy.

It was at this point that we were having so much trouble getting a male. It began to look as though N'Pongo and Nandi would have to end their days as virgin spinsters, a thought that was naturally abhorrent to us. It was then that Ernst Lang offered us Jambo. This was an enormous piece of luck from many points of view. Lang had been the first person in Europe to breed and successfully rear a gorilla, the famous Goma, and since that remarkable breakthrough (for gorillas were one of those difficult beasts that it was said could not be bred in captivity), his gorilla family had gone from strength to strength. Jambo was one of the males born into the family. Not only was he zoo bred, but he himself was the father of a young male, the mother of which was his sister. This meant that Jambo was no callow teenager whose knowledge of sex was confined to perverted peeps at the health and strength

95

magazines; he was a fertile male who knew how to mate.

This is very important, for there are many things in the apes' world that are learnt by example and successful copulation seems to be one of them. An ape reared without contact with a herd seems to be singularly inept and, in some cases, a totally unsuccessful lover, simply because he was never shown. Jambo had not only been shown by his enormous father, Achilla, but had proved that he had paid proper attention to the demonstration. His final qualification was that he was just the right age to become N'Pongo's and Nandi's husband. Lang had extolled his virtues in letters and, rather in the manner of the early royal marriages, photographs had been exchanged. We were told that Jambo was exceptionally powerful and exceedingly handsome, black but comely and with a rather humorous expression. We all thought he was perfect. Now we had to wait to see if the two females agreed.

Introducing animals is a heart-stopping business. Will they attack each other and if so, will the hose pipes, the buckets of water, the pitchforks, be of the least avail? If not, will they simply ignore each other, or will they ignore each other to begin with and then attack each other later, when one has been lulled into a sense of false security? If they do ignore each other, does this mean that they might grow to like each other later on, or were all one's trouble and expense in vain? Anybody who cherishes the idea that all individuals of the species are bound to be alike in given circumstances, should have been there to watch the introduction of Jambo to N'Pongo and Nandi. It was a classic in every sense of the word.

We had confined the females in one of the three sections of the bedroom so that, through the barred divisions, they could look into the third bedroom into which we were going to release Jambo. Between the male and the females would lie a section of the bedrooms and two sets of bars. This would, we felt, act as a buffer-state, until we got some idea of all three participants' reactions to the whole idea. N'Pongo and

96

Gambar, a Sumatran Orangutan, 'one of the most intelligent apes
I have ever had the privilege of meeting'.

Jambo, an exceptionally powerful gorilla, 'black but comely and with a rather humorous expression'.

Nandi could tell something curious was going on by all the untoward activity, but they had no idea what, since Jambo was still invisible in his travelling crate.

The moment arrived, the slide on Jambo's crate was lifted, the door to the bedroom slid open and Jambo, massive and black as coal, reeking with the garlic-like smell of gorilla sweat, swaggered, hunching his shoulders like a professional heavyweight, into the cage. He gave one swift, all-embracing glance around him, saw the females, but made no sign. He squatted for a moment to gaze around him in a lordly fashion before starting a slow perambulation around the bedroom, examining every nook and cranny with interest, but still totally ignoring the two females. The effect of all this on the females was fascinating. Both of them, when they heard the slide, had come forward and peered, but when Jambo saun-tered, dark and handsome, into their line of vision, the reaction of each one was totally unexpected by us.

We had thought that, if either of them displayed immedi-ate interest, it would be the basically friendly, extrovert N'Pongo. Nandi always tended to be suspicious and kept herself to herself. But the moment Jambo strolled into view, N'Pongo took one good look at him and then turned and walked off, showing by the set of her broad back a measure-less disdain. She expressed quite firmly a total lack of interest in the opposite sex and Jambo in particular. The effect on the anti-social Nandi was quite different and charmingly comic. She was a little way away from the bars, squatting on her haunches, when Jambo came into view. She took one look at the massive shape and reacted in much the same way as a teenage girl might if her favourite pop star suddenly walked into her bedroom, clad in nothing but a guitar. The expres-sion on her face was one of incredulity and wonder; nothing in her previous life had prepared her for this miracle. No one had told her that such a thing as a handsome male gorilla existed. She took one look at Jambo and fell instantly and irrevocably in love.

I am sorry if this sounds unscientific and anthropomorphic,

but in the dry and pedantic jargon of the biologist there is no way to describe it. She shuffled her way to the bars, never taking her eyes off this wonderful apparition, and clung on to them in a rather desperate sort of way, gazing wide-eyed and immobile at the apparently disinterested Jambo. She sat in a trance, drinking in his every movement. Once, during the course of investigations, he disappeared behind the wall for a few moments. Her distress was immediate; she ran to and fro, trying to see where he had gone. Eventually, when he did not reappear, she came to the conclusion that he had gone out through the slide into the outdoor area. Instantly she ran to her own slide, bent down and tried to peer under it. Fortunately for her peace of mind, Jambo reappeared, nonchalantly sucking a piece of orange and ignoring Nandi's display of uncontrolled passion. Relieved to see him again, she once more took up her station at the bars and gazed at him reverently and adoringly. N'Pongo, meanwhile, had eaten a few nuts, peered out of the window at us and finally lain down on her shelf, utterly ignoring the presence of a male in their midst.

When they were finally allowed in with each other, both females carried on in much the same way. It was obvious that N'Pongo, for so many years the queen of all she surveyed, viewed the newcomer with suspicion and jealousy but with a certain caution too. She decided to continue her policy of pretending that the eighteen-stone Jambo did not exist. Nandi, on the other hand, behaved, if possible, in an even more inane manner now that she could get close to the object of her passion. She would squat within a foot or so of him, gazing at him raptly, her eyes shining with affection. After a time, when Jambo lay in the sun and allowed her to groom him, her joy knew no bounds and she would lean up against his massive body, with a look of besotted pride on her face that was so human it was laughable. N'Pongo was somewhat distressed by this liaison, but she still maintained her domination over Nandi. However, there now developed an unfortunate association between N'Pongo and Jambo.

Jambo, for all his experience, was still very young and full of what can only be described as youthful high spirits and crude humour. He knew N'Pongo disliked him and this aroused in him a sort of devilment. He would practise all sorts of schoolboy pranks, which, as we know, can become very wearing to the nerves. He would jump out on her suddenly when she least expected it, or, sauntering past, would suddenly rush at her and pull her hair. Immediately N'Pongo would attack him and he would run off. This teasing would go on until N'Pongo was in a towering rage and would pursue him, screaming abuse, accompanied by Nandi who, rather half-heartedly, took her part. But it was obvious that Nandi would consider such attentions from Jambo as a pleasure and privilege and was somewhat puzzled by N'Pongo's reaction.

Jambo, of course, like all practical jokers, did not know when to stop. He never actually hurt N'Pongo, except for a few minor bites and scratches (nothing by gorilla play standards), but as soon as he found that he could make her lose her temper, he teased her unmercifully. N'Pongo began to have the hang-dog air of the wife of a professional humorist and, what was worse, she started to lose condition. Reluctantly we had to separate her from Jambo, allowing them into the outer areas separately, and dividing Nandi's time between the two so that Jambo would not get bored and N'Pongo not become too jealous.

Then N'Pongo came into season and suddenly it was vouchsafed to her what a male gorilla, even an irritating practical joker male gorilla, was for. With complete shamelessness she would solicit him through the bedroom bars and, when allowed in with each other, copulation took place almost at once. During the whole time she was in season, N'Pongo tolerated Jambo. Although she did not display quite the hero worship of Nandi, she nevertheless abandoned herself to the carnal delights in the most whole-hearted fashion. Then, the moment she was out of season, she resumed her former relationship with Jambo. Once again they had to be separated.

99

Though she became more tolerant of Jambo as the months passed, she still only really had time for him when she was in season. It would have made things much easier for us if she had lived in harmony with him, but we had to be thankful for small mercies. At least she had mated with him and that was the main thing. Nandi, too, had received his attention when in season and so now all we could do was wait and hope that both females would be fertile, give birth successfully and, most important, prove to be good mothers.

At long last, from the latest batch of urine samples that had been sent off to the laboratories, came back the exciting news that both females were pregnant. The first one to give birth was Nandi. This, our first gorilla birth, was a never-to-be-forgotten occasion. Apart from the importance of the birth itself, gorillas have only been bred since the 1960s and only forty-seven of them have been reared successfully. We hoped that there were going to be no complications because it was Nandi's first baby. With the aid of a closed-circuit television we had installed in the den, a twenty-four-hour watch was possible and thanks to this we noticed that Nandi was starting her labour at eight o'clock one night. Operation Gorilla came into force at once.

Over the months, as Nandi and N'Pongo had grown more and more rotund, we had been making our preparations to try to cover all eventualities. We could not assume that both gorillas were going to be good mothers, nor could we assume that the births were going to be easy and normal; so everything, from the possibility of having to do a Caesarean section to taking the babies away and hand-rearing them, had to be taken into consideration and planned for.

The most likely event was that we would have to remove Nandi's infant and hand-rear it. This being so, a room in the Manor was prepared as a nursery. It had a built-in airing cupboard, wash basin and cupboard space, and in this room were installed our two Oxygenair baby incubators and, for use when the babies grew older, large wickerwork clothes' baskets to act as sleeping quarters and a play-pen. The nursery was heated by a thermostatically controlled radiator and kept at between 70° and 75° F. As well as this, we installed a washing machine for nappies and a tumbler clothes dryer. In addition, of course, we had to lay in a stock of oddments ranging from baby oil, baby lotion and nappies, to feeding bottles, thermometers and plastic pants. In spite of the fact that the outlay had .been considerable, we hoped we would not have to use any of it.

By the time Nandi started to strain at eight o'clock that fateful night, we felt we had taken every precaution that was humanly possible. Now it was up to Nandi and we could only watch and be ready to help, should it be necessary.

It was a nerve-racking time. From the moment we noticed the first straining until the moment Nandi had the baby in her arms, took nine hours and twenty-four minutes – an unprecedented length of time according to the observations we had of gorilla births in other zoo collections. The baby was what is known as a ventex presentation – that is to say it was born face downwards instead of face upwards – and, as such, it inevitably produced an unnaturally prolonged labour. There was one point (when Nandi had already beaten the record for the longest labour so far observed) when we seriously and reluctantly started thinking in terms of a Caesarean section, but we eventually decided against it, as Nandi, although in pain and restive, was in good physical condition. We decided to wait, for a Caesarean section is not an operation you undertake unless you have to. Luckily Nandi gave birth before reaching the time limit we had set.

From the commencement of labour until the moment of birth, every move that Nandi made was recorded; a total of 260 observations, which make up one of the most comprehensive scientific coverages of a gorilla birth ever made. Nandi cleaned up the baby very well and then ate the placenta and membranes. She held the infant close to her body and with great tenderness, so we had high hopes that all was going to be well. But then we came up against the usual stumbling block. Nandi had no idea that the baby should feed. Four hours after birth, the baby, a male, tried to suckle, but was pulled off the nipple by Nandi.

The maximum recorded time that a baby gorilla had been left with its mother before being removed for hand-rearing was thirty-two hours, but our baby was so strong and so eager to feed that we left him with Nandi for forty hours. Still she would not let the infant suckle. Reluctantly we loaded the capture-dart gun, tranquillized Nandi and removed the baby. This was taken up to the nursery (beautifully decorated with cut-out pictures of Walt Disney characters on the walls and ceiling, so that the babies' eyes would have something to focus on) and installed him in the incubator. The baby's first few feeds, which he took greedily, consisted of glucose and water; after that he was started on Dextrose and rapidly gained weight. We christened him Assumbo after an area in the Cameroons, which is the most westerly part of Africa in which Lowland Gorillas are found. He proved to be an exceptionally good baby.

Three months later, it was N'Pongo's turn. Unfortunately, she gave no preliminary signs that she was going to commence labour and, as we had had several dates recorded as possible birth dates, we were taken by surprise. The first we knew of it was at eight o'clock in the morning, when our Curator of Mammals, Quentin Bloxam came on duty and found N'Pongo sitting on her shelf, totally ignoring her baby, which was lying on the floor, waving its arms about and whimpering. N'Pongo had eaten the placenta, cleaned up the baby and then, feeling that that was the extent of her obligations to the future of the gorilla race, had placed it on the floor and left it to its own devices. Quentin opened the slide leading into the outside area and N'Pongo walked past the squealing infant without even a glance and went outside. It was obvious that, as far as she was concerned, it was now up to us. Quentin rescued the yelling baby and it joined Assumbo in the next-door incubator. It proved to be a male as well, so we christened it Mamfe, again after a place in the Cameroons which I had used as a base camp on my collecting trips in West Africa.

The two boys grew apace and eventually graduated from incubator to basket and play-pen and (when they got too boisterous) to a cage in the Mammal House. Here, with access to sunshine and fresh air, they grew even quicker, beating up their toys and thumping their chests like adult gorillas in an effort to prove to us how powerful and savage they were, a boast belied by their enchanting woolly, picca-ninny looks and the humorous glint in their eyes.

They had hardly settled down in their new quarters when the nursery was filled again, for, once more, Nandi and N'Pongo, within a few weeks of each other, had their second infants. Once more, we had unfortunately to take them away. Nandi's second baby was a female, called Zaire, and was the cause of much rejoicing, for in gorilla births in captivity there has been, up to now, a preponderance of males. N'Pongo's second offspring was a male, Tatu, probably the handsomest baby we have yet had and the image of his father. As I write this, Nandi is pregnant for the third time and I have no doubt that N'Pongo will follow suit. If these two births are success-ful, it will mean that we will have had six gorillas in three years, which cannot be considered bad going by any standards, when you remember that the first gorilla birth was recorded in 1956, just under seventeen years ago and that there have only been seventy-four successful births to date. It is to be hoped that we can keep at least a trio of these or subsequent youngsters, to form a potential breeding group for the future, when Jambo and N'Pongo and Nandi are past breeding age. The object of the exercise is to have our breeding groups self-sustaining, so that not only will it be unnecessary to catch gorillas in the wild again, but, from our breeding pool, we will be able to supply other zoos.

Chapter Five

'This beast has a stone in its eye, also called an Yena, which is believed to make a person able to foresee the future if he keeps it under his tongue. It is true that if an Yena walks round any animal three times, the animal cannot move. For this reason they affirm that it has some sort of magic skill about it.

'In part of Ethiopia it copulates with a lioness, from whence is born a monster known as a Crotote. This can produce the voices of humans in the same way. It is said not to be able to turn its eyes backward, owing to its rigid backbone, and to be blind in that direction unless it turns round. It has no gums in its mouth. It has one rigid tooth bone all the way along, which shuts like a little box, so that it cannot be blunted by anything.'

T . H . W H I T E – *The Book of Beasts*

'In much research wild animals are the raw material of zoology and their continued existence for this reason is essential. We still have much to learn about our own evolution, behaviour, diseases and, above all, our own relation to the natural environment. Man has the power to control nature to a certain extent, but equally he is part of nature and in order to understand himself completely, he can only do so in the context of nature and wild animals.'

C A R O L I N E   J A R V I S –
The Value of Zoos for Science and Conservation

'Pythagoras says : "Serpents are created out of the spinal marrow of corpses" . . . And this, if it is to be credited, is all very appropriate : that just as Man's death was first brought about by a Snake, so by the death of a man a snake should be brought about.'

T . H . W H I T E – *The Book of Beasts*

Fables, Facts and Files

It is obvious that the human race is still woefully ignorant of how the world works. In many parts of the planet, we are destroying with such ferocious rapidity that there is not even time to give a name to or scientifically to describe what we are destroying, let alone to discover its importance, biologically speaking. It is as well to remember that, when we exterminate a species, we endanger or destroy with it a host of satellite creatures that depend upon it for their existence. When you chop down a tree, you are not just killing a tree, you are destroying the equivalent of a vast and teeming city, because there are so many different forms of creature that live upon it. What we are doing can have far-reaching effects; effects which may not be apparent on the surface; effects which ultimately may rebound upon mankind in an unpleasant way. People comfort themselves with the old saying : 'You can drive nature out with a pitchfork, but she will return'. The word to note here is 'pitchfork'. When pitchforks were the most up-to-date weapon in man's armoury against nature, this was, of course, true; but now you are driving nature out with pesticides, bulldozers, chain-saws, man-made floods and man-made filth – relentlessly, thoroughly and speedily, so she cannot return.

I get very tired of people asking me what *use* are the animals I am trying to preserve? What use can some obscure tropical creature be to a man in Sydney, or Chicago, or Stalingrad, or Peking?

The answer comes in two parts. First, we have no shred of moral right to exterminate a species which has taken millions of years to evolve and which has as much right on this planet as we have. In fact, it has now more right to be here, since it has not tried to step outside its allotted place in nature and is, in most cases, of benefit to its environment in consequence. This cannot be said of so-called civilized mankind, however sanguine your view of your own species. Second, if one must adopt the arrogant and God-like attitude that a thing should only exist if it is of use to man (that chapter in Genesis has a lot to answer for), then the reply to 'what use are they?' is simply that, as yet, we have not the remotest idea of what is and what is not of benefit to mankind.

There are thousands of examples which show clearly how, first of all, we have to know how the world functions, before we can manipulate it to our benefit, without destroying it; and how the most obscure and unlikely creature may turn out to be of enormous use to us. Let us take just three.

In England, the county of Sussex was famous for its white clover and, indeed, large numbers of people depended upon this crop for their livelihood. Then the clover suddenly and mysteriously started to fail and whatever the farmers did was of no avail. In desperation, as a last resort, they turned to a biologist for help – something they should have done in the first place. That they happened to choose a man called Charles Darwin was fortuitous. Having investigated the problem, Darwin informed the worried farmers that what they wanted was more cats; a remark which led the stalwart sons of the soil to believe that the old boy must have taken leave of his senses.

It appeared that there was only one sort of Bumble bee which had a proboscis long enough to fertilize the rather complex clover flower. This bee built its nests in the banks in the hedgerows. A species of Field mouse lived in the banks; a rodent with a sweet tooth, who would dig out the bees' nests and eat the honey and the young. It appeared that the Field mice were having a population explosion and the number of natural predators had not risen sufficiently fast to cope with this. The rodents' depredations on the bees' nests were becoming so great that the results were showing in the poor clover crops.

In Brazil, they decided that it was silly to have such an important crop as the Brazil nut scattered about the forest in the untidy way that nature had arranged. It was obviously more sensible to grow them in rows in plantations, like any other crop. This was done, and the trees grew, prospered and flowered, but to the mystification of all they produced no nuts. Belated investigation disclosed a situation somewhat like the Bumble bees and the clover. Apparently the flower of the Brazil nut tree has been adapted so that it can only be pollenized by one species of bee, which has strength enough to raise a kind of trap-door to get into the flower. Now this insect found that on a plantation it had no nectar to feed on when the Brazil nut tree was not in flower, so, not surprisingly, it ignored the unnatural plantations and remained in the forest, where it had a sufficient supply of food all the year round.

Then there is the case of the humble armadillo – a sufficiently obscure animal, you would have thought, to have been useless to a human being anywhere, except possibly for food, or (in the case of the Paraguayans) for making guitars out of their skins. However, it seems possible that this inoffensive creature may prove to be of enormous use to mankind. Experiments suggest that the armadillo could help in the eradication of leprosy. This creature, perhaps because it has an extraordinarily low body temperature, is the only one in which the human *Lepra* bacillus proliferates in sufficient amounts to be potentially useful in the creation of a vaccine against leprosy. Furthermore, it is believed by cancer researchers that the study of leprosy patients will provide them with the knowledge as to why people suffering from cancer fail to reject their tumours.

It should be clear from these three examples, that what we are basically in need of most urgently is knowledge of how our world functions.

If you ask the average person what they think a zoo is for, the majority will reply, 'for entertainment', and a few will say, 'so that we can study animals'. For zoos to have got themselves branded as a form of entertainment, like Bingo and horse-racing, is entirely their own fault, since they have, in the past, spent too much time behaving like circuses and too little time studying the animals in their care or keeping records of their research. In fact, if museums had behaved in the irresponsible and wasteful way with their material that zoos have done, they would have been closed down years ago.

The purpose of keeping any collection of wild animals in confinement should be threefold : first, to conduct as complete as possible a biological study of every species, especially those aspects which are too difficult or too costly to study in the wild and which may help in the preservation of that species in its natural habitat; second, to aid severely endangered species by setting up, under ideal conditions, protected breeding groups and, eventually, a reintroduction programme, so helping to ensure their future survival; thirdly, by the display and explanation of this work to the public, to persuade people of the vital necessity and urgency for the overall conservation of nature.

From point one – the careful and comprehensive study of a collection of living animals – should emerge material which will be of great value to conservation, both protected breeding programmes and conservation in the wild state, and a wealth of information which will be of biological and educational value. The extensive scientific study of its living creatures, therefore, should be the prime objective of any zoological garden or other collection of wild animals. The amassing of this data should be as wide and as detailed as possible; it should then be correlated, evaluated and the results published so that other organizations may benefit from this harvesting of observations and conclusions. Unless this is done, there is no justification for keeping collections of wild creatures; unless all the points outlined above are adhered to by a zoo, it merely becomes that pathetic, archaic and useless thing, the nineteenth-century menagerie or sideshow.

It would seem to be totally unnecessary to underline these simple, basic facts, but the truth is that all over the world a disproportionately large number of zoos have been woefully neglected in the past (and still are today) in what should be their *raison d'être*. In far too many collections, the record system is either non-existent or distinguished only for its primitiveness and the paucity of the information it contains. Let us be clear on this; one would not expect science in the fairground, circus or other zoological extravaganza, but one does expect a modicum of it in any reputable zoological garden or other collection of wild animals that lays claim to be anything other than a sideshow.

I think it is impossible to emphasize too strongly that one can accomplish more by the study of biology in a properly run zoological garden than in the best of museums, for the simple reason that one is dealing with an unlimited canvas, presented to you by live animals, and not the, by and large, rather limited one presented by the dead remains of that animal. Yet it is a sad fact that only a handful of zoological gardens have been utilized in this way for proper scientific research.

In 1963, when the Trust came into being, I was determined that, from the outset, we would create a scientific record system which, I hoped, would grow in scope and importance as the Trust's activities expanded. Over the years, I had communicated with many zoos in all parts of the world about their record systems and, in many instances, had seen them at first hand. In all but a few cases, where a record system existed at all (and in most cases it did not), it was worse than useless. So we were forced to start from scratch, which, in many ways, was probably just as well.

The planning stage, in creating such a record system, is fraught with difficulty. What looks innocent and straight-forward on the surface suddenly takes on the aspect of a Gordian knot tied by an inebriated octopus. Eventually, how-ever, and not without considerable acrimony and hesitancy, we laid down the following basic structure. It was evolved after much hard work and thought on the part of the manage-ment committee and members of the staff, who, after all, were the ones who had to run it and maintain it. While trying to avoid the pitfall of over-simplicity, we also tried to circum-navigate the abyss of over-complication. An over-complicated and cumbersome record system, whatever gems of information are embedded in its labyrinthine ways, is a useless thing. It must be a tool that can be used by everybody.

We also tried to foresee our needs, feeling that one com-prehensive record system seemed preferable to ten separate ones, whilst realizing, resignedly, that ten separate ones would one day grow, amoeba-like, from our first attempts. This has proved, to a certain extent, to be true. For example, on our behaviour card we decided to include a space for photo-graphic and sound recording references, which would event-ually, we knew, evolve as a separate file. At that time the Trust was in its infancy and so desperately short of funds that it made both these references seem an unnecessary, even a grandiose and slightly lunatic, inclusion. Recently, however, we have been able to make a start on our photographic file and we hope that sound recordings (to enter the, as yet, almost untouched field of animal vocalization) will, when we can afford it, become a reality and not just an unfilled space on a card. By including these at a time when they were no more than visionary, we had a cross-reference ready printed into the card and therefore did not have to reprint the entire card to include them at a later date.

We started with three major cards, covering history, medical record and behaviour. The cards measure 11½ by 8¾ inches and are in three different colours for quick reference: white for history, pink for medical and blue for behaviour. To save time, the top section of all these cards is identical and contains the basic seed information, such as age, date of arrival, condition, the all-important zoo reference number, etcetera.

The history card contains all the information we can acquire about the newly arrived specimen and as much data on its habits in the wild as is known, so that this can act as a guide for the person looking after it (should he or she be unfamiliar with the species) and help the newly arrived or trainee member of staff.

The medical card is filled with details of any veterinary treatment the animal receives while it is in the collection and has a section for the eventual autopsy report.

The behaviour card should, perhaps, more correctly be called the ethological card. This contains any observations on the specimen's behaviour, from such things as courtship display to gestation periods and the development of the young.

It is almost inevitable that there will be some repetition on these cards. We found, after some years, that it was necessary to add a breeding card for the mammals, since otherwise the details of breeding had to be entered either under behaviour or medical, both of which might cause confusion. At the same time, however, courtship displays, or gestation periods, or any medical treatment for the pregnant female, could be added to the correct card as well. For the birds, we found it was extremely helpful to evolve an egg card. These have been most useful in working out percentages of successes at the end of the breeding season. It was due to the introduction of these cards that we have noticed what we suspect to be a dietary deficiency among some of the birds, which we are in the process of investigating.

At the back of the mammal and bird files, we have appendix cards, which are pink in colour. The information on these ranges through anaesthetic, nutrition, gestation periods, and hand-rearing longevity periods. These are for a simple, quick reference. At the front of the mammal and bird files are four cards on which are registered arrivals, trades, losses and breeding. Again, these are simply for quick reference. These are all the large cards and they contain all the detailed information about the specimens, but for quick reference overall, there is a small card index, which is in alphabetical order, for mammals and for birds. These cards measure 4 by 5 inches and contain a résumé of each individual animal, its movement and its reference number. For a quick overall picture of the individual specimen, the small reference cards are used. From there we can find the zoo reference number of the creature concerned and look it up on the other, bigger, more detailed card for whatever facts we wish. The reason we found this card index necessary was because, on the large cards, we keep the animals in the reference order, that is to say, the order in which they arrive or are born, and under the zoo reference number. In the card index system, to speed the process of searching, we keep them in alphabetical order.

Just recently, we had to start four other filing systems. The first was the bibliography file. This cross-references authors and subjects, and contains details of all the articles written by members of the staff, both for our Annual Report and for other scientific journals. Then there is a file on nutrition, which gives what is known about the animal's wild diet and its diet in the collection. We hope to expand this file considerably as our nutritional research progresses. There is a veterinary index. This is just a simple file cross-referencing species and diseases, so that we can see at a glance which species have had what diseases. Finally, there is a photographic file, which is arranged alphabetically under species. When I write it down like this the whole system sounds incredibly cumbersome, but it is in fact basically very easy to use. It takes a secretary only an hour a day to keep the references up-to-date on all the cards.

The material for this filing system is accumulated from the all-important Day Diary, which is kept in the office of Jeremy Mallinson, our Zoological Director. In this, every single item

Baby gorillas receiving attention: *above* Assumbo held up by the Consultant
Paediatrician to test his reflexes and *below* Bamenda 'imitating as part of a
series of psychological tests'.

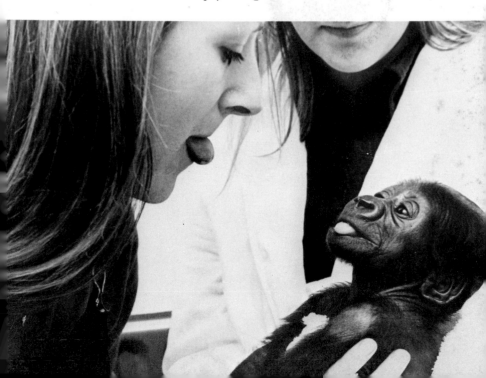

Tatu, N'Pongo's second baby and probably the handsomest yet reared in the Zoo, being bottle fed and exercising his teeth.

appertaining to the care of the animal is entered daily : behaviour patterns, the laying of eggs, the gestation periods, and so on. These are then typed on to the appropriate cards by the secretary.

As the collection expands, of course, inevitably yet other files will have to be set up, but for the moment, we find that the present system, though perhaps not perfect, is at least efficient. Our records go back over twelve years and we have already managed to extract some valuable information from them, as our Annual Reports show.

We work on the principle that it is better to over-record than under-record. This means that every conceivable thing is noted down, including a lot of perhaps unnecessary information, which has eventually to be winnowed out when it is written up as an article. When dealing with animals on this scale, you are never sure which observations are going to be of value. Therefore it is better to have everything noted down so that it can be evaluated and sifted at leisure, rather than to find gaps because something was not noted as it was considered unimportant at the time.

The thoroughness with which we try to document even the simplest thing is well illustrated by the cards covering the operation of moving our two female gorillas a distance of about 100 yards, from their old cage into their new quarters. On the face of it, the job appeared to be a simple one of sedating two animals and, while they were unconscious, transporting them from point A to point B. But there was much more to it than that. To begin with, there was considerable risk involved, for a dose of anaesthetic that will immobilize one gorilla, might well kill another one, even if it were of the same age and weight. The period in which we had them unconscious provided an ideal opportunity to examine their teeth, take blood samples, measure and weigh them and do the host of things that we could not normally do, in spite of their comparative tameness. But the whole operation had to be conducted with speed, smoothness and efficiency, so that there would be no risk of the gorillas recovering half way through our investigations. We were anxious that their recovery from the anaesthetic should not be unnecessarily delayed and that there should be no risk of them catching cold. Pneumonia, after anaesthetic, is a common complication that can be fatal.

Firstly, we noted down the various pieces of equipment that were needed, the general procedure and who would be in attendance :

MOVEMENT OF LOWLAND GORILLAS
FROM OLD TO NEW ACCOMMODATION
29th February, 1972. N'Pongo M.1+ Nandi M.2+

Provisions and Equipment in Readiness for Move.
1. Two APS stretchers (loaned from the St John's Ambulance Brigade).
2. Two blankets.
3. 30 ft binding rope.
4. Weighing Scales (loaned by the Animal Shelter).
5. Oxygen Cylinder.
6. Wood wool (wood wool beds have been made under both shelves in new cage).
7. Tape measure.
8. Den area of new cage has been checked over and found to be in working order. F. temperature of den 65-68 degs. Both shelves warm to touch. Slides all working.
Mr T. B. Begg, MRCVS, and a General Practitioner to be in attendance.
General examination of both specimens to be carried out, including examination of teeth.
Blood sample from each specimen.
Each specimen to be weighed and measured.
Sgt McLinton from the States Police Force, and fingerprint expert to take three sets of fingerprints from each specimen's *right* hand. This information to be sent to the International Gorilla Studbook holders in Frankfurt, and also used for comparative studies.

Full documentation and photographic record of move to be carried out.

14.20 hours. Lower Mammal House to be closed to the public.

Movement of Specimens: –

Once it has been established that both Gorillas are sufficiently sedated to move from cage, the following procedure will come into effect :

1. Each specimen to be carried out manually on to a waiting APS Stretcher in mammal house corridor.

2. Once laid on stretcher, gorilla to be covered with blanket up to neck, and binding rope used to secure specimen on stretcher.

3. Each specimen to be weighed in mammal house.

4. N'Pongo to be taken to No. 1 den (north side). Nandi to be taken to No. 2 den (south side).

5. Blood samples, fingerprints, measurements, and general examination should take place in the new accommodation, the priority being to get the move completed as quickly as possible.

6. The gorillas will be kept separated and both will be prevented from getting into the middle den area until they are completely back to normal state.

Staff in Attendance : – Jeremy J. C. Mallinson, J. J. Mallet, Q. M. C. Bloxam, P. F. Coffey, D. V. Riordan, J. Usher-Smith.

14.30 hours. Each specimen to be given orally 300 mg. Sernylan (Phencyclidine) (3 ml. of 100 mg. strength). Gorilla weights estimated at approx. 75 kgs. (165 lbs.). The above dosage was administered in milk/honey/Vit. B.12.

Information continued on a separate card for each specimen. N'Pongo Sheet 4, M.1. Nandi Sheet 4, M.2.

Then the animals were sedated. One can see from the notes that they reacted in different ways. These rather cold and precise observations, of course, do not record that each and every one of us had our hearts in our mouths (unscientifically speaking), though we all tried to adopt the nonchalant air of people who move gorillas every day of the week. The most important point was, of course, that these were not just animals; they were our personal friends and we did not want to lose them.

29th February 1972

MOVEMENT TO NEW ACCOMMODATION
'N'Pongo' Zoo Ref. M.1. Sheet 4.

14.30 hours. Sernylan administered. 14.31 Great agitation shown by both specimens when no food was administered. 14.45 Specimens appear to be calmer. 14.46 N'Pongo pulled herself on to shelf with slightly more effort than usual. 14.52 N'Pongo's eyes looking dull. 14.55 N'Pongo swaying on perch. 14.55½ N'Pongo moved from standing on all fours to sitting position, head hanging down. 14.56 Very unsteady. 14.58 N'Pongo collapsed into a lying position, sat up again, very unsteady. 15.01 On the floor. 15.02 Collapsed, face and body to the floor, hind legs slightly tucked up underneath her. 15.03 Nandi ran past her and hit her on back. N'Pongo reacted by moving slightly. 15.05 Nandi hit N'Pongo again. No reaction from N'Pongo. There was no further reaction or movement from N'Pongo after 15.05. N'Pongo = 35 minutes.

Tuesday 29th February

MOVEMENT CONTINUED NANDI M.2

14.30 Sernylan administered. 14.31 Great agitation shown by both the specimens when no food was administered. 14.45 Specimens appear to be clear. 14.50 Nandi's eyes appear duller and slightly sunken. 14.55½ Nandi showing great agitation, rushing at slide and banging it. 14.55 Nandi displaying threat posture, still very agitated, continuing to run at slide and bang it. 14.57 Nandi salivating more heavily. 14.59 Nandi continuing to display threat posture and great agitation. 15.03 Nandi ran past N'Pongo, hit her on back. 15.05 Nandi hit N'Pongo again. No reaction from N'Pongo. 15.06 Nandi not totally steady but appears to be strong and aware. 15.07 Nandi less agitated and active. 15.07½ Nandi yawned, supported herself by leaning buttocks against wall, still on all fours. 15.08 Head slumping, body swaying. 15.09 Nandi sat down. 15.10 Nandi's eyes closing. 15.11 Nandi lurched a few steps forward then collapsed into similar position as N'Pongo. 15.12 Nandi lifted head and lowered it again. There was no further reaction or movement from Nandi after 15.12. Nandi = 42 minutes.

As soon as they were both unconscious, we swept into action. The stretchers were taken into the cage and the gorillas strapped to them. They were brought out into the Mammal House corridor, where they were weighed. After being taken to their new accommodation they were then measured; swabs, blood samples and fingerprints were taken and their teeth were examined. Though none of us said anything, I think we all felt that, although we recognized it was necessary, it was unpleasant to see animals we knew so well (always so bright and alert, so full of personality) lying flaccid and unconscious while their mouths were opened and peered into, swabs taken, their blood sucked from their veins. We felt it was somehow an invasion of their privacy, an undermining of their dignity, and we were glad they would know nothing about it afterwards. In other words, we felt thoroughly anthropomorphic and unscientific about it.

They were swathed in blankets and a procession of us moved out of the Mammal House, carefully carrying this precious cargo, looking not unlike a worried group of people bearing the only survivors from some awful catastrophe. They were carefully bedded down in lots of straw (separated from each other, but close enough to be able to see each other when they recovered) and we gathered around to await their return to consciousness. This was, perhaps, the most nerve-racking time, for it was now we would see whether they would emerge from the anaesthetic without mishap.

Again, these clinical observations give no hint of our state of mind. We smoked, we drank cups of coffee, we endeavoured to discuss the current world crisis, but, inevitably, the rather desultory talk would die away until there was only the deep stertorous breathing of our patients. We were all remembering N'Pongo's arrival as a baby : tiny and fat, black as coal, her mouth curved in a perpetual smile, calmly accepting that all humans were friends : of Nandi's arrival, when she disliked and distrusted humans, a great scar – a machete slash – across the top of her scalp explaining the reason for her antisocial attitude, and how we had patiently and triumphantly won her confidence over the years. We had known them since they were babies : we could not be entirely detached and refrigeratedly scientific.

Observations: – At 4 o'clock N'Pongo was beginning to react – turned her head and chewed her lip.
16.48 N'Pongo moving around, unable to stand but rolling about. 18.00 Moved from bars lying on stomach towards centre of cage. 18.30 Lying on her stomach, supporting herself on her elbows, looking around dozily. She got up on her haunches, supporting herself on bars, fell over, then crawled towards heater. 19.00 Moved nearer heater, some small amount of arm movement. Lying on stomach in hay. 19.30 No change in position to above. 20.00 Much more alert – sitting half upright can lift head to vertical, responds to name. 20.08 Back in old position on bars. 21.30 Moving around floor on all fours, limbs hardly supporting her weight. 22.15 Lying on stomach no reaction to noise. 22.50 sitting up – evidence of vomit around mouth – focusing though still groggy – shivering slightly. 24.00 Little change – lights switched off.

Observations: – Nandi, when brought out of old cage, was coughing and salivating, yawning and blinking.
18.00 Nandi lying in middle of floor face down. 18.30 Has moved slightly and has hay and wood wool around

head and shoulders. 19.10 Lying on hay – head in hay – no movement, breathing easily. 19.30 Moving around on all fours, but very unsure. Responds to her name. Smelling paintwork and rapping knuckles on floor. Sitting on her haunches, breathing is a little strained. 19.55 Showing interest in food – bit into orange, moving actively, falls over on occasions, but keeps moving even after falling on back – gets up straight away. Some nasal discharge. 20.00 Nandi climbed bars, hangs for $3\frac{1}{2}$ minutes. 20.10 Tried to be sick once – saliva dribbling from mouth. 20.15 Nandi actually vomiting. 20.19 Trying to vomit again. 20.20 Trying to vomit again. 20.27 Nandi drinking warm milk/10% Glucose solution – no co-ordination – drinking with upper lip first. 20.31 Nandi standing hooting and drumming on her chest. 20.33 Again standing drumming chest and hooting then sitting – more prolonged hooting. 20.35 Drinking again. 21.50 Nandi on shelf – co-ordination much improved, calmer. 22.15 Sitting on shelf, walking around on shelf. 22.45 Appears to be asleep. 23.30 On shelf – resting/sleep posture – quite alert. 24.00 On shelf, resting appears calm – lights off.

This simple moving operation meant that we now had the exact weights and measurements of the two apes, a breakdown of their blood, a complete bacteriological picture of each specimen from the nose, throat and vaginal swabs, and a lot of information on the use of tranquilizers and anaesthetics. We had done, in fact, a thorough check on their physical well-being, in a way that would have been impossible otherwise, even with such comparatively tame specimens. All this went into the filing system for future reference.

So much for science. When it was over, I opened some champagne – I felt we needed it.

Of course, consistent and detailed records are invaluable in veterinary and parasitological research. A good example of how parasitology in veterinary science is sometimes inextricably entwined is our mournful series of cards on the Volcano rabbits. Mournful, because it reposes in the dead file awaiting resurrection when we obtain some more of these fascinating little creatures. The minute and exceedingly rare Volcano rabbit is found only on the extinct volcanoes surrounding Mexico City, Popocatepetl and Ixtaccihuatl. Although they are strictly protected, like so many other things, it is paper protection only; they are hunted and killed, regardless of the legislation covering their well-being, even in the place where you would have thought that they would have received some sort of sanctuary, the Popocatepetl National Park. Here the forest guards assured me that they ate them. This being so, and the range of this interesting animal being so limited, it seemed the sort of species which was in need of help from our Trust. So in 1968, I financed and led an expedition to Mexico, during which the acquisition of a breeding colony of the Volcano rabbits was the main objective.

I met with great courtesy and help from the Mexican authorities and, after three months, returned to Jersey successful. We had acquired six rabbits and we found that they seemed unperturbed by the journey and settled down very well. We were even successful in breeding them, which was the first time in captivity and a great triumph. But then our trials turned to disaster : we lost our only male specimen and a port-mortem revealed that it was suffering from a form of coccidiosis. After some anxious weeks, we managed to obtain another male from Mexico, but before he could be introduced to the females, he also died. The post-mortem result was the same and was of great interest, for it seemed that the animal not only brought with it a new disease, but a new species of disease.

The fact that we now knew the enemy of the Volcano rabbit and how to combat it was of no avail, for I had no reliable contact in Mexico who could procure me the rabbits to found another colony. But I live in hopes of one day returning to Mexico and obtaining more rabbits, so that we can get this unique and fascinating little animal firmly established under controlled conditions.

It is curious that many people overlook the basic fact that to protect and conserve an animal in the wild state, you must not only know how it functions but its inter-relationships with a multitude of other species. To put it simply, there is no earthly use in setting aside 5,000 square miles of savannah for the preservation of lions, if the area contains no antelope. If you have not established by observation (either in the wilds or captivity) that a lion is carnivorous, then your conservation work is doomed to failure. Whilst it is obvious that animals must be studied in their natural state for this purpose, it is undeniable that there are certain things it is easier to observe, and certain things that can only be observed, where the creature is living under controlled conditions.

Let us take two examples : firstly, our files on the breeding of the Tenrecs. These strange little hedgehog-like creatures come from Madagascar. One of their many endearing characteristics is their habit, when picked up, of pulling the loose skin down over their foreheads towards their noses in a ferocious, scowling frown of disapproval. We have successfully bred these little insectivores to the fifth generation and their progeny have been sent all over the world. From our breeding records has emerged a host of observations on behaviour, numbers of young, parturition and so on – all information that would be costly, time-consuming and, in some cases, impossible to obtain from the wilds. Many of the things we have recorded can help with the conservation of other species of Tenrec. There are twenty-five named forms (some of them extremely rare) and with our experience of two comparatively common species (the Pygmy and the Spiny hedgehog) we hope, in the future, to be able to establish breeding colonies of the rarer and more endangered ones.

From our work with the common species, for example, we discovered that we could manipulate the Setifer species by temperature control. They were kept between 80 and 85 degrees Fahrenheit, dropping to 70 or 75 degrees when the animals were undergoing their equivalent of hibernation. By manipulating the temperature and humidity it was found that we could keep Setifers active all the year round and thus in breeding condition. Using this method, we have been able to make the female capable of conception at two months (whereas breeding in the second season has hitherto been the rule). This way she could have two to three litters a year, without hardship. If techniques like this could be applied to the endangered forms, it would be of enormous value in building up large, viable breeding colonies, as an aid to their conservation. This is an example of the type of material a well-run animal collection should be able to amass and the use to which it could be put.

A second example of the type of useful material you can obtain comes from the files on our African civet colony. From our original stock of two, we have, to date, bred forty-nine of these and exported twelve to four zoological collections throughout the world. From our breeding records, we have worked out gestation period, probable longevity, normal number of young and their development, weight increase and growth measurements, notes on mating behaviour, parturition, and so on. In fact, we now have a complete picture of the normal breeding behaviour of the African civet, consisting of material which would have been difficult, if not impossible, to provide by field work alone.

Just recently, there has been a wave of anti-zoo feeling and propaganda, both in Europe and in the United States. The scientific critics of the zoological garden condemn them for their lack of scientific work. In all too many zoological collections, this is only too well justified. Sometimes, in the ones that *do* attempt to keep records, the results are so pathetic that no responsible biologist could be expected to look upon them with anything but scorn. We have in our files, for example, a card from a well-known zoological garden, giving details of veterinary treatment for a giraffe. It merely states that, after a dead calf was removed from the female by the veterinary surgeon, the animal was 'then injected with antibiotics'. No mention is made of the quantity nor, indeed, the type of antibiotic used and the entry is hand-written, so it could be illegible to any stranger looking to it for information. From cards we received from another collection, we saw that an animal arrived and that it died, followed by a most detailed pathological report. No behaviour was recorded, so we got the impression that the animal did not do anything at all between its arrival and its death. We were left with the strong impression that the zoo concerned was merely a sort of waiting-room for the pathologist.

In 1968, four years after we had started the Trust and our record system, there was a big conference in San Diego on the role of zoos in wild life conservation. At it, Caroline Jarvis (now Lady Medway) who was then editor of the *International Zoo Year Book,* made what I considered to be the most forthright, intelligent and constructive speech at the conference. Dealing with the threat of extermination facing so many species throughout the world today, and the role of zoos in conservation, she said :

'In this situation, zoos have a very important part to play, though few of them seem to realize it. According to the most recent records of the *International Zoo Year Book,* there are row about half a million wild vertebrates living in about five hundred zoos and aquaria. The significance of this huge figure is twofold : it indicates the scale on which zoos are involved with wild animals and it means that zoos are more closely concerned with wild animals than any other type of organization. They have more immediate contact and are familiar with a wider range of creatures. They have more opportunities to record certain kinds of data and knowledge available to them than any university, research institute or game department. This is why zoos are particularly so important, both to conservation and to zoological research. Conservation depends on knowledge, zoological research depends on knowledge and it is knowledge that is at present locked up in such vast quantities in zoos. Nature has been described as a treasure house of knowledge, and zoos are the caretakers of a considerable part of it, but only too often they are unaware of their responsibilities as caretakers, or even that they are caretakers at all.'

Dealing with the importance of zoos in the accurate collection of information, Miss Jarvis went on to say :

'Apart from education, there are two other supremely valuable things that a zoo can do to help save the world's animals from extinction. The first is to record wild animal data and the second is to breed endangered species in captivity. One of the main difficulties of wild animal conservation is the lack of knowledge about the basic requirements of the creatures we are trying to protect. It is astonishing how little is known about the biology and behaviour patterns of the majority of wild animal species, for relatively few studies in depth, such as Schaller's justly famous work on the Mountain gorilla, have been made. Much of this necessary information, such as the animal's relationship to its environment, the ecology of its habitat, its natural diet and many of its behaviour patterns admittedly can only be studied in the field, but at the same time, there is a great mass of data, impossible, or extremely difficult, for field workers to acquire, which can most easily be obtained by studying animals in captivity. Until very recently, zoos seem to be largely unaware of the immense amount of valuable information that is available to them and of the importance of this information, if it is accurately recorded. Only a few zoos have good record systems going back over many years and even in these zoos, the amount of information recorded is meagre and sometimes inaccurate.'

In dealing specifically with record systems, she said :

'If information recorded by zoos is to be valuable, it must be much more extensive, much more methodical, much less haphazard than it is at present and two things are essential; a good record system and efficient techniques for animal identification. The records need not be complicated, but they must be accurate and precise. All zoos should record a basic minimum of data on their wild animals, preferably on a card index system, listing every individual, identifiable animal in the collection, the date of its arrival, its estimated age and weight on arrival and the locality where it was obtained, its identifying marks, its sex, date when it mated or gave birth to young, dates of any illness during its lifetime and the date of death or departure and the cause of death and departure.'

After this conference, Miss Jarvis wrote an excellent short paper published by the Zoological Society of London, entitled *Guide to the Study of Wild Animals in Captivity*. Judging by our knowledge of the filing systems still employed by the majority of zoos, this invaluable publication has not had the wide distribution that it deserves.

It was, however, nice to realize that, seven years after we had started our record system, Miss Jarvis was suggesting that other zoos should do just what we had done. We were pleased to notice that we had covered every aspect that was alluded to in her speech.

If they wish to avoid or mitigate the wave of criticism now being levelled at them, zoological gardens and other collections of wild animals must display a much more responsible attitude towards their role as scientific institutions. It is a disturbing thought that, over the years, thousands upon thousands of animals have been kept – and are still being kept – for no other purpose than to amuse the public and that we have learnt – and are learning – nothing from their incarceration.

Zoological parks and gardens, scientifically and intelligently run (the terms are not synonymous), are going to be of increasing, not decreasing, importance in the years to come. They will probably be the last refuge of a vast number of species. It is therefore of the utmost importance that they efficiently keep, breed and *observe* the animals in their care. They are the guardians, the preservers of the other animal species that are attempting to share this planet with us, in most cases with conspicuous lack of success.

Let us not forget how recently it was in our history that we worshipped animals (in some parts of the world we still do) nor how recently people believed in unicorns, that a toad had a jewel buried in its head, that swallows spent the winter hibernating in the mud at the bottom of ponds. In his brilliant book, *The Folklore of Birds,* Edward A. Armstrong quotes an example of 'scientific investigation', which, in our history, is comparatively recent :

> In the second half of the seventeenth century we find John Aubrey writing : "Sir Bennet Hoskins, Baronet, told me that his keeper at his parks at Morehampton in Hereford-shire, did for experiment sake, drive an iron nail thwert the hole of the woodpecker's nest, there being a tradition that the damme will bring some leafe to open it. He layed at the bottome of the tree a cleane sheet, and before many houres passed the naile came out and he found a naile lying on the sheete. Quaere the shape or figure of the leafe. They say the moonewort will doe such things. This experiment may easily be tryed again."

Such were the ideas of country gentlemen less than two hundred years ago. These educated men were curious, interested in experimentation, but casual as to method and credulous as to the result. John Ray replied forthrightly :

> The story . . . is without doubt a fable, yet this eminent naturalist blamed the death of his daughter from jaundice on the use of new-fangled scientific remedies instead of the old-fashioned cure – beer flavoured with horse manure.

Of course, since then, we have gained enormous knowledge of how animals behave and of the ecology of the world in general, but what we must realize is that, vast though our knowledge has become, it is still infinitesimal compared to what has to be learnt. Because we pluck a star out of the sky, it does not mean to say that we understand the universe.

Finally, I must say this : a record system is only as good as the people who devise it; it is the people who inherit it that must make it grow, graft on it, rearrange and nurture it and, where necessary, kill it and start again. The important thing about our record system is that everyone on the staff, qualified and unqualified, contributes his observations and so do all concerned with the day-to-day keeping of the animals. This is what makes their observations of such importance. It is clear that in a collection like this it is no use having a white-collar, office-bound scientist who only sees the animals once a month and relies almost entirely on other people's observations. It must also be remembered that one must not work on the assumption that the people who contribute the data are omniscient. However desirable omniscience might be, it is not something acquired by experience, a religious upbringing or even a university education.

One can only go on the principle that, in the country of the blind, even a white stick is a start towards the acquisition of knowledge.

Chapter Six

'Weasels are said to be so skilled in medicine that, if by any chance their babies are killed, they can make them come alive again if they can get at them.'

T. H. WHITE—*The Book of Beasts*

'Violet most amiably knitted a small woollen frock for several of the fishes, and Slingsby administered some opium drops to them, through which kindness they became quite warm and slept soundly.'

EDWARD LEAR

'Herba Sacra. The "divine weed", vervain, said by the old Romans to cure the bites of all rabid animals, to arrest the progress of venom, to cure the plague, to avert sorcery and witchcraft, to reconcile enemies, etc.'

BREWER'S *Dictionary of Phrase & Fable*

Pills, Potions and Palliatives

The discovery, identification and subsequent curing of an illness in animals is a task so fraught with difficulty that it might have made even the stout heart of Florence Nightingale quail. Imagine a patient who not only cannot tell you where the pain is, but, in many cases, takes great care to cover up all its symptoms; a patient who, having decided that you are trying to poison it, refuses all medication, regardless of how carefully embedded in meat, banana or chocolate it is; a patient who (because you cannot explain), interprets everything you do, from X-ray to injection, as a calculated assault on its life, its dignity, or both. With sick animals, you find that you have to have the patience of Job, the grim determination of Sisyphus, the duplicity of Judas, the strength of Samson, the luck of the devil and the bedside manner of Solomon before you can hope to achieve results.

A collecting expedition (where you have to be carpenter, dietician, cage cleaner, cook and veterinary surgeon to your animals) teaches you a lot about the basics of dealing with animal ills. When you have a collection of several hundred animals to look after and you are 140 miles away from the nearest settlement (which probably does not boast a doctor, let alone a vet) you have to develop your own approach. It does not, of course, have the delicate insouciance of Harley Street and, if the British Medical Association could see you at work, it is probable that you would never survive the strictures laid upon you.

After all, what respectable member of Harley Street would muffle a reluctant and, in consequence, greatly impassioned patient (in this case a mongoose) in an old plimsoll so as to give it an enema with a scent spray, purchased (in desperation) in the local native market? What dedicated Harley Street specialist would disrobe himself before an audience of some 200 fascinated Africans and prod himself all over with a hypodermic syringe, in order to persuade a highly suspicious (and immensely powerful) baboon that this was a most desirable and fashionable experience? What fastidious Harley Street man would consign himself, for the sake of his calling, to bed with a young chimpanzee (suffering from bronchitis) who spent the night trying to start gay romps, poking his finger in one's eye, or urinating copiously, and with immense satisfaction, every half hour? What slick, sleek, product of Guys, Barts, Edinburgh or University College is troubled by the danger that his patient may peck him up the left nostril while he is attending to a broken arm? This happened to me while I was setting a Tiger bittern's wing, and the agony and resulting gory mess were hardly compensated for by the knowledge that the bird had missed. It was aiming for my eye.

I do not wish to seem harsh in my attitude towards the medical profession, but they really have a rather cushy job compared to someone who has to deal with animals. I defy any ordinary GP not to tear up his diploma when faced with thirty-seven monkeys, all suffering from acute diarrhoea brought on by an African animal boy feeding them Cascara tablets in place of their normal Brewers' yeast : this ten minutes before you are due to put them on board a ship whose captain is notoriously anti-animal. But exhausting though this sort of training is, it gives you a good grounding in what to expect thereafter. And so, when you meet with a success in animal nursing, you are generally surprised and gratified.

The techniques for dealing with an animal in the back of beyond and dealing with one in a well-run zoo are similar, but not identical. For many years, there has been much argument in zoo circles as to the desirability of hospitals for animals. There are two schools of thought. The first maintains that a sick animal should be removed from its fellow creatures so as to prevent the spread of disease, to enable it to recover in hygenic surroundings and to ensure that the veterinarian dealing with it has it under the controlled conditions which are best from his point of view. The second argues that, although a hospital may be necessary for providing the hygenic conditions needed for an operation, the psychological effect on the animal of its removal from familiar surroundings into unsympathetic and strange-smelling ones as well as the loss of its familiar human contacts and its being put in charge of a stranger, is more detrimental than its quick return to unhygenic but familiar safe quarters. Of the two schools of thought I favour the second one. The effect of a serious illness on an animal is psychologically shattering in itself. Add to this the inevitable fear created by the process of medication or surgery, and add to *that* the removal of the creature from its own known and comforting territory and human contacts, and you are much more liable to have an animal which will panic or depress itself into death.

In the early stages of the Trust's existence, the thorny question of whether or not to have a hospital was purely academic as far as we were concerned. We simply had not got the money to construct such a facility and therefore had to take a third line, which both schools of thought on the hospital problem tended to overlook. As we had not the wherewithal to create a hospital, it was up to us to try to eliminate, so far as was possible, the need for one. That is to say, by spending what money we had on the provision of the .best possible food and the most comfortable accommodation, we tried to practise what could be called a form of preventive medicine. To a large extent, we found that this *does* work. Our incidence of illness, considering the size and scope of the collection, has been extraordinarily light. But this is not to say that we have been totally free. We have had our quota of illnesses, epidemics and accidents from what the insurance companies (who always love laying the blame at other people's doors) call 'Acts of God'.

Our lack of facilities, however, did cause many problems for our long-suffering veterinary surgeons. A major abdominal operation is fraught with danger in any circumstances. To have to perform it in a place where you cannot provide perfect aseptic conditions makes things much worse. To keep your patient like that after the operation doubles your chances of failure.

Our first experience with this came when a lioness, who was almost ready to have her cubs, picked up a gas-forming organism. Naturally when she started her labour, it became impossible for her to give birth. We were in a difficult position, for the animal would take no anaesthetic by mouth and, at that stage in our career, we were so poor we could not afford the luxury of the Capchur-dart gun. The whole thing was made more difficult by the fact that it happened over a week-end. I had to get my friend, Oliver Graham-Jones, then the chief veterinary officer of London Zoo, to give up a pleasant weekend pottering round his prize rose bushes so as to fly to Jersey with his Capchur gun (he could not let anyone else do the job, as the police insisted that only he had a permit to use it). With the aid of our own veterinary surgeons the lioness was immobilized and we prepared for the Caesarean section. The operation took place in the open air part of the cage, with some old dentists' spotlights set up for illumination. The operating table was striking in its simplicity; a well-scrubbed, ancient door on two trestles. It says much for the skill of our veterinary team that the already suppurating cubs (three of them) were removed and the lioness sterilized, with no complications of pneumonia or peritonitis, in spite of the fact that, after the operation, the zoo workshop had to double as a recovery hospital.

Unhygenic though this operation was, however, it is necessary to point out that there are times when you can be too hygenic. If you scrub out your animal's cage with disinfectant clear that in a collection like this it is no use having a white-twice a day, disinfect its food, keep it carefully segregated from the public and wear mask and gloves yourself when in contact with it, the animal may thrive; but let one small, determined and unpleasant bug wriggle its way past your defences, and you will have a dead animal on your hands, for it will not have built up the resistance to counteract it.

A good example of this was the case of our two baby gorillas, Assumbo and Mamfe. The successful breeding of gorillas is still a sufficiently unusual occurrence to make the event notable and so these two – our first births – were treated with considerable reverence. Their nursery was most hygenic, their nappies hygenically washed, their food hygenically pre-pared, everyone who dealt with them or visited them wore masks and they were guarded from infection as if they were heirs to some holy dynasty. Then came the day when they had outgrown the incubator, the laundry-basket beds, the play-pen and, finally, the nursery itself; so they were trans-ported in triumph down to the Mammal House, where a special cage had been prepared for them.

Almost immediately, Mamfe, the younger of the two, be-came ill. At first, he merely displayed a fluctuating interest in his food, a certain lethargy and a small weight loss. When this was accompanied by diarrhoea as well, Dr Carter, our local paediatrician, who had kept the infants under his care from birth, was sent an urgent call. His initial report (en-shrined in our files and published in our Eleventh Annual Report) states that :

'Examination at the time confirmed the lethargy and loss of appetite and he was not keen to play with Assumbo; how-ever the tongue was clean although slightly dry; the throat was clear and no abnormality could be detected in the lungs. There was no evidence of any lymphadenopathy, the cervical, axillary and epitrochlear glands were all normal nor were the inguinal glands enlarged. Examination of the ears and throat showed no evidence of inflammation and urinalysis performed in the Laboratory showed no evidence of any urinary tract infection. Mamfe was treated empirically with Lomotil (Searle) 2.5 ml. three times per day (Diphenoxylate hydrochlor 2.5 mg. atropine sulph. 0.025 mg. in 5 ml. suspension). It was noted that he tended to vomit after the administration of Lomotil and he was kept on clear fluids such as 5 per cent glucose solution and diluted S.M.A. milk.'

However, the diarrhoea continued and when the laboratory report came through on faeces culture, it showed a pure growth of E. Coli. This is an unpleasant infection which can be a killer. The laboratory informed us cheerfully that it was sensitive to Chloramphenicol, Tetracycline, Streptomycin, Septrin and Neomycin, but this did not help much. It was a Saturday afternoon (why do animals always get sick at a weekend?) and there was great difficulty in getting a choice of antibiotics. Mamfe was therefore given Oxytetracycline, 125 mgms. in syrup, every six hours. This, to our increasing alarm, did not reduce, or stem, the diarrhoea. When Dr Carter came in on the Sunday, Mamfe was in bad condition and severely dehydrated. Dr Carter's report continues :

'He was listless and barely responded to human touch; his eyes were sunken and had a glazed appearance and he was disinterested in his surroundings and often did not appear to be focusing his eyes. The eyeballs were sunk into the sockets and he gave the typical appearance of a seriously dehydrated human baby. His tongue was dry and the skin on his abdomen was lax and when picked up between finger and thumb and then released, the elevated skin did not fall back as readily as normal. It was apparent that emergency measures were required to resuscitate the infant as soon as possible. When any restraint was used, he found reserves of strength. No attempts to give intravenous fluids could be made and so three different techniques were employed : –

(i) *Intra-peritoneal transfusion.* This method was described and used extensively by Carter (1953) in Africa as a method of rehydration for acutely dehydrated babies and the infants very rarely made more than a token protest at the procedure. However, Mamfe reacted very vigorously and by his continual shrieking, he raised his intra-abdominal pressure to such an extent that it was considered that the gut might be in danger of perforation by the needle. The needle was therefore withdrawn after 50 ml. of Hartmann's solution had been administered and other routes were then used.

(ii) *Sub-cutaneous infusion into the thighs.* It was noted that Mamfe had very lax skin lying over the antero-medial aspects of his thighs and it was decided to try this method previously used extensively in paediatric practice in Children's Hospitals, combined with hyaluronidase 150 oin. dissolved in 500 ml. Hartmann's solution. It was found that 80 mls. of Hartmann's solution could be injected with ease into the sub-cutaneous tissues in the antero-medial aspects of both thighs and it was quite astonishing to see the rate at which the fluid was absorbed in as much as it looked as if twice the quantity of fluid could have been administered in this way, if necessary.

(iii) *Tube feeding.* As Mamfe had not been troubled by vomiting apart from immediately after the administration of Lomotil, it was decided that this route should be attempted. It was calculated that he would require another 180 ml. of fluid to reach an approximate fluid balance in view of his state of dehydration. Miss J. Robbins, S.R.N., S.C.M., whose hospital duties routinely included tube feeding premature human babies, passed a gastric tube through the mouth with such speed and ease that Mamfe never even attempted to gag. 180 ml. of clear Hartmann's solution was administered slowly by tube. In addition, Mamfe was given an intramuscular injection of Ampicillin 50 mgms. and Cloxacillin 25 mgms. in the form of Ampiclox (Beecham) six hourly for the following few days, and Miss Robbins instructed the staff at the zoo on the technique of tube feeding. Within a short time, the passing of the oro-gastric tube was done without any difficulty whatsoever. Further therapy required by Mamfe is given elsewhere, but dehydration had been successfully overcome and never became a problem thereafter.'

The infant gorilla, so plump and exuberant one minute and shrivelling away to nothing the next, was a sight not to be forgotten. Dr Carter told me that this was a fairly common occurrence in premature babies who, once they were removed from the carefully controlled environment of the intensive care unit into an ordinary ward, frequently became a prey to E. Coli and had little resistance to it.

Naturally you have to take all sensible precautions to prevent infection. Our policy is that every new arrival should be segregated while all possible tests on it are carried out, before it takes its place in the collection. By this means you minimize or eliminate the chance of introducing a sick animal. If the animal shows signs of disease, or of internal or external parasites which might contribute to disease, it undergoes treatment and is segregated, until it is no longer a danger. Thus we try to safeguard against a disease being introduced by a newcomer. It is for this reason that we have had to give up treating oiled or sick wild birds, for we found they were introducing parasitic infections through our defences. We now send them to the island's equivalent of the RSPCA and give advice and help at long range, should it be necessary.

Quarantine periods and tests are our first line of defence, but we realize, ruefully, that this is not impregnable. Take the dreaded disease, aspergillosis, a virulent fungus that thrives in the lung cavities of birds and for which there is no known cure. There is a lot of evidence to show that a bird may live for years with a low grade infection of this without showing any signs. But should the bird undergo any stress, such as being caught up to be removed from one aviary to an-

A Tenrec, a strange little hedgehog-like creature from Madagascar.

Canadian Eagle-owl chicks.

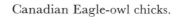

We like to allow the baby gorillas access to the public.
Here Mamfe meets a new friend.

Vets carrying out
an examination of
a sedated leopard.

Hand rearing a
baby Saddleback
Tamarin.

The author with Princess Anne, Patron of the Wildlife Preservation Trust,
on the occasion of her visit to the Zoo.

other or to be sent away, then the disease will flare up and kill the specimen in a short space of time. Owing to the fact that, in many instances, the disease is undetectable, what appears to be a healthy bird will suddenly, for no apparent reason, die. Only on post-mortem, does one find that its lungs are quite literally a fungus bed of infection. The chances of this happening with a newly arrived bird are, of course, considerable. As I have said elsewhere, one of the cock White-eared pheasants had this disease on arrival and died within twenty-four hours. With the White-eared pheasants we have bred in Jersey, we have had the same problem. We sent them away, apparently in tip-top condition, then heard that they had died of aspergillosis within twenty-four hours of arrival. Obviously they were infected before they left us, but showed no signs.

A still more unhappy example of the way an animal can appear hale and hearty and then suddenly reveal that it is suffering from a deadly disease, is provided by the case of Oscar, our male Bornean orang-utan. We had procured Oscar when he was a tiny baby. During his childhood he had had the normal round of coughs and colds, but had contracted nothing serious. Eventually he grew into one of the most magnificent orang-utans I have ever seen, with the wide, fleshy picture-frame of his species surrounding his face, from the middle of which appeared his small and sagacious eyes. Oscar was enormous; as strong as two men and apparently in the pink of condition. Then, one day, he seemed to be listless for no obvious reason. Four days later this powerful and apparently healthy animal was dead.

The decline started with a lack of interest in his food. This could, of course, have been attributed to anything, from the start of a cold to toothache, but, on the rare occasions when we do get some symptoms from an animal, we always find it safer to assume the worst. As is usual practice with our apes, both our veterinary surgeons and our doctor were therefore called in. Oscar was given what treatment they could mete out, but, with such scanty evidence, it was difficult to diagnose from what he was suffering.

On the second day, he started having diarrhoea and from then on, he went steadily downhill. Our predicament was that we could not immobilize him for examination, for the speed with which his condition deteriorated made the risk of killing him too great. So it came to the last day, as it is recorded on our cards:

Wednesday, 25th July

12.15 a.m. Specimen sounds as if he is coughing slightly.

12.40 a.m. Specimen vomited very little fluid.

1.30 a.m.–3.15 a.m. Specimen very restless during this period, not sleeping very much and moving position frequently. Stomach contractions have been occurring at infrequent intervals, but only one observation of actual vomiting. His eyes are very bright and he appears to be alert.

3.55 a.m. Turned over on to side, stomach contractions and wind.

4.10 a.m.–5.40 a.m. Slept fairly well with occasional changes of position. Resp. 21-22 per min.

5.40 a.m. Became quite alert, sat up leaning on uprights of platform. Offered drink but did not accept.

5.45 a.m. Lying on back dozing, with periodic grunts.

5.55 a.m. Turned over on to side, then on to stomach. Responded to gentle talking. Soft grunts. Offered drink. I thought he was going to accept half, sat up then settled down again.

6.00 a.m. Sleeping soundly. No stomach contractions visible.

6.50 a.m. Woke up. Came very weakly to bars. Took two mouthfuls of liquid containing Keflex. Gradually slipped off bars down to floor.

7.05 a.m. Shaking/trembling.

7.12 a.m. Resp. 20.

7.50 a.m. Resp. 24.

9.15 a.m. On back – noise with every breath, mouth open.

9.20 a.m. Convulsions, terminal vomit.

138

The post-mortem was kindly done for us by Dr John Cragg, the Director of the States of Jersey Pathology Laboratory, and it was discovered that Oscar had been suffering from ulcerated colitis – a condition fairly rare in human beings and even more so in orang-utans. The mucous membrane of the bowel is attacked and ulcers form which, eventually, cause death. It was startling to find from the autopsy that Oscar must have had this condition for some time, but had displayed no signs of it, for parts of the colon were regenerating, indicating that the large bowel had started to heal, when the disease proved fatal.

It was small comfort to realize that such an obscure disease could not possibly have been diagnosed from the slight symptoms that we could observe, nor that, when the disease is diagnosed in humans, the treatment is the insertion of a cortisonal enema – a process which requires the co-operation of the patient for success. Oscar, immobilized, could not have helped in this. An Oscar fully conscious, certainly would not have co-operated.

Compared to human medicine, veterinary surgery is still in the middle ages. We are lucky in having not only intelligent, but interested veterinary surgeons looking after the Trust's collection; but, by and large, I have met with more ignorance about wild animals among veterinary surgeons than in any other class of human being, with the possible exception of zoo-keepers, zoo directors and biologists. Face him with any-thing from a Fennec Fox (smaller than a miniature poodle) to the giraffe of the dog world, a Maned wolf, and the average veterinary surgeon will insist on treating the two animals as if they were Retriever puppies out of the same litter. Structur-ally speaking they are both dogs, but a wealth of difference lies between them, not only in size, but in habits, habitats, and psychology. I suppose it is not to be wondered at since, during the course of their rigorous training, veterinary surgeons rarely, if ever, see anything other than a domestic animal. There is little incentive to tiptoe into the unexplored and dangerous regions of veterinary surgery dealing with wild animals.

There is a huge field of research open in wild animal veterinary surgery. In years to come, when if we behave with intelligence we may be farming such esoteric things as Eland, Giraffe, Blackbuck or Anoa in a desperate attempt to keep at least some humans alive, a knowledge of exotic veterinary surgery will be of immense use. So little is known about wild animals that anything achieved can be counted as an advance. Take artificial insemination, widely, and to a large degree successfully, used with domestic animals. Its use with the rare wild animals is still in its infancy, but sufficient work has been done to show that it might be a major conservation tool in breeding threatened species. At Cornell University, for example, a breakthrough has been made in the artificial insemination of Hawks and in a project for returning captive-bred eggs to wild nests (the eggs from which, coming from parent birds infected with insecticides, are either infertile or soft-shelled, and the young often born deformed). Thus, hopefully, such things as the Peregrine Falcon may be reintroduced to areas in which it has suffered the fate that Rachel Carson predicted in her book, *The Silent Spring.*

In the field of nutrition, there are great advances to be made, for without knowledge of the correct nutritional requirements you cannot hope to keep or breed wild animals successfully. Will the addition of mushrooms to a diet make the difference between success or failure in breeding? Or moss? Or seaweed? Or is one simply feeding too much?

Our ignorance is vast. We know little, for example, of stress factors, which may range from the fact that the public is too close to the animal, to the fact that another animal of a different species is in the next cage. In our new Marmoset and Tamarin Complex, inadequate ventilation in the corridor between the inside bedrooms is causing a stress problem, though at first sight this may seem ludicrous to suggest. The reason is that these little primates mark their territories with their pungent, musky scent glands, rubbing them on the branches or wire of their cages. In an inadequately ventilated area, they can, of course, easily smell the territory markings of the different species that surround them. This makes them feel that their territory is threatened and so, frantically, they mark their cages twice as much, but to no effect.

If, in the future, a great proportion of the world's wild life will exist only in the zoos, then it is of the utmost importance that we should solve, or at least try to solve, as many of these problems as possible. At such a time zoos will be handling even rarer species and, with these remnants, we cannot afford to take risks. We should approach such veterinary problems with the same whole-hearted enthusiasm as is now devoted to the problems of such things as the cow, the sheep and the horse. The latter, after all, are in no danger of extinction.

Chapter Seven

'With a hazard of these dimensions looming ahead one might expect that our species, unique in the animal kingdom for its capability for logical anticipation, would already be caught up in a near-frenzy of conservationist activity. In reality it is difficult to find a single public warning, much less any sign of action . . . This is no fanciful excursion into science fiction : given a continuation of present trends it is probably the most optimistic way of speaking of man's future. When the swarming stage is reached in nature, mass mortality is inevitable . . . Perhaps those who anticipate the end of the road in this way are wrong, and some way out can be found. If so, it can only be through an unimaginable transference of our total scientific effort from exploitation to conservation. It is certainly to be hoped that those who have plumbed the depths of pessimism will not cease to urge constructive action along these lines in order to try to avert what they feel to be almost inevitable.'

DR S. R. EYRE – *Population, Production and Pessimism*

'The Four Travellers were therefore obliged to resolve on pursuing their wanderings by land, and very fortunately there happened to pass by at that moment, an elderly Rhinoceros, on which they seized; and all four mounting on his back . . .

'Thus, in less than eighteen weeks, they all arrived safely at home, where they were received by their admiring relatives with joy tempered with contempt; and where they finally resolved to carry out the rest of their travelling plans at some more favourable opportunity.

...'As for the Rhinoceros, in token of their grateful adherence, they had him killed and stuffed directly, and then set him up outside the door of their father's house as a Diaphanous Doorscraper.'   EDWARD LEAR

> 'In the midst of the word he was trying to say,
> In the midst of his laughter and glee,
> He had softly and suddenly vanished away –
> For the Snark was a Boojum, you see.'
>
> LEWIS CARROLL

142

The Stationary Ark

I hope that in this book I have done a number of things. Above all, if you are anti-zoo, I hope I have shown that well-run zoos are an aid to animals and are not detrimental to their well-being; that, indeed, in many cases, zoos will turn out to be the last refuge of numerous species in a human-being-infested world.

However, having said that then I must agree with you (if you are anti-zoo), that not all zoos are perfect. Of the 500 or so zoological collections in the world, a few are excellent, some are inferior and the rest are appalling. Given the premises that zoos can and should be of value scientifically, educationally and from a conservation point of view (thus serving both us and other animal life), then I feel very strongly that one should strive to make them better. I have had, ironically enough, a great many rabid opponents of zoos tell me that they would like all zoos closed down, yet the same people accept with equanimity the proliferation of safari parks, where, by and large, animals are far worse off than in the average zoo. An animal can be just as unhappy, just as ill-treated, in a vast area as in a small one, but the rolling vistas, the ancient trees, obliterate criticism, for this is the only thing that these critics think the animals want.

It is odd how comforted people feel by seeing an animal in a ten acre field. Safari parks were invented purely to make money. No thought of science or conservation sullied their primary conception. Like a rather unpleasant fungus, they have spread now throughout the world. In the main, their treatment of animals is disgraceful and the casualties (generally carefully concealed) appalling. I will not mention the motives, or the qualifications of the men who created them, for they are sufficiently obvious, but I would like to stress that I know it to be totally impossible to run these vast concerns with a knowledgeable and experienced staff, since that number of knowledgeable and experienced staff does not exist. I know, because I am always on the look-out for such rare beasts myself.

I am not against the conception of safari parks. I am against the way that they are at present run. In their present form, they represent a bigger hazard and a bigger drain on wild stocks of animals than any zoo ever has done. Safari parks, properly controlled and scientifically run, could be of immense conservation value for such things as antelope, deer and the larger carnivores. But they have a long way to go before they can be considered anything other than animal abattoirs in a sylvan setting.

I feel, therefore, that one should strive to make zoos and safari parks better, not simply clamour for their dissolution. If Florence Nightingale's sole contribution, when she discovered the appalling conditions in the hospitals of the last century, had been to advocate that they should all be closed down, few people in later years would have praised her for her acumen and far-sightedness.

144

My plan, then, is that all of us, zoo opponents and zoo lovers alike, should endeavour to make them perfect; should make sure that they are a help to animal species and not an additional burden on creatures already too hard-pressed by our unbeatable competition. This can be done by being much more critical of zoos and other animal collections, thus making them more critical of themselves, so that even the few good ones will strive to be better.

It is an extraordinary thing that you can trace zoos back as far as China more than two thousand years ago and the fantastic collections of the Aztecs in South America, when it was first discovered by the Conquistadores. Zoos have been going strong, in one form or another, since the first primitive man walled up his first Giant sloth in a cave. Yet legislation covering zoos is infinitesimal.

In Great Britain, for example, subject to local council approval, anybody can start a zoo. Once he has got his collection of animals together, the proprietor is answerable only to the local health authorities for the cleanliness (and they worry more about cafés and lavatories than they do about cages) and to the local RSPCA in terms of cruelty to the animals. Now, this organization does a good job, but apart from the more obvious signs of ill-treatment (such as an animal covered with sores, or with its ribs sticking out through starvation), the inspector is pretty helpless. He has not had any training with wild animals. What, on the face of it, may look perfectly adequate, could be, from the animal's point of view, the most monstrous cruelty.

After the last war, there was a sudden mushroom upsurge of ill-kempt, badly-run zoos, created by a variety of unqualified people. I was once phoned up by one of these mushroom zoo directors, who wanted some advice. He had a cage, 12 ft by 6 ft, and he wanted something to fill it. His problem was that he not only did not know what anything was, but he did not know the size of it either, so he asked me to translate several available animals' names for him (such as cougar, hyena, blackbuck, etc.) and for me to give him the dimensions of these various available animals to see which species would conveniently fit his cage. God knows, you have to have a licence for practically every other activity! Should you not be required by law to prove some competence before you are allowed to start a zoo? It is curious that this situation should exist in a country whose people never tire of telling themselves and others what fervent animal lovers they are.

Some time ago, the responsible zoological gardens in Great Britain started the Zoological Garden Federation. Its objectives were to try, by inspection and suggestions, to raise the standards of animal husbandry, zoo design and techniques. We became a member of the Federation, because we considered that, as there was no Government control, there ought to be some standards set and adhered to, if only by the zoos concerned. This group of zoos imposed these restrictions upon themselves, so the Federation, within its framework, did a very worthwhile job.

Its next stage was to try to get a Bill through Parliament which would at least produce a measure of control over existing zoos and set standards for any future ones. It was on the make-up of this Bill that the trouble started. It was suggested, quite rightly, that there should be set up an impartial Government body to inspect and control zoological gardens, and to have some measure of control over the sort of people who started them. Among other very necessary regulations, it provided that all zoos should keep records of their importations, births and losses and that this Government body should have access to such information. Predictably, perhaps, the majority of the purely commercial zoos violently objected to this. In an effort to try to prevent the Bill from going through Parliament, they formed an opposition body called the Zoological Gardens Association which included most of the safari parks. The object of the exercise was, of course, to try to form an association including a greater number of organizations than the Federation had in its ranks, so that they could then turn to the Government and say they were the representative voice of the zoo world. This would, of course, have enabled them

146

either to squash the Bill entirely, or else to make sure that it contained no teeth – was no more than a sanctimonious Government cloak under which, and because of which, they could continue as before, while blinding all critics with the newly acquired integrity conferred on them by the Bill.

Fortunately, the Federation stuck to its guns and apart from a few minor alterations, insisted that the Bill should be as planned. I personally think it was not nearly tough nor searching enough, but it would have served very well as a start. However, the Government, faced with two separate bodies who did not seem able to agree on what they wanted in the Bill, or indeed whether they wanted a Bill at all, simply made a Levantine moue and said, in effect, 'mend the breach in your ranks, decide what Government control you want, and then bring your Bill back'. There is now some sort of a move afoot to endeavour to control zoos by local authorities. I suppose that would be better than nothing, but if you are, say, the Duke of Dulally and the biggest landowner in the district and you happen to have turned your stately home into a safari park, I wonder how many minor public officials would have the courage to tell you that you were maltreating your animals or, indeed, to put any sort of curb on your activities. It is really a most unsatisfactory state of affairs.

Until one has Government control, the best way of achieving an improvement in zoo standards is for zoo visitors to ask questions when they go to an animal collection and to be gently persistent (following their queries up by letter and telephone if necessary) until they get a satisfactory answer. Here are some very rough guidelines on what to look for and what to ask. (I do hope, incidentally, that you will apply this method to us, should you visit Jersey. I assure you we are far from perfect.) This tiny aide-memoire applies to *all* zoos and *all* collections of exotic animals *anywhere* in the world. It can be roughly divided into two parts : what to look for, and what to ask.

Look for the condition of the animal (ignore the cage to begin with). Look for an air of contentment – glossy and tight

The Reptile House

feathering in birds; sleek, shiny coats on well-covered bodies in mammals; a healthy patina on reptiles, amphibians and fish. Above all, look for that unflurried, relaxed air of happiness : it is quite unmistakable when you see it.

(*Remember that new arrivals, oldest inhabitants, or sick creatures can look like hell*).

Look at the cage. Remember that, in many cases, the size is not all that important (unless miniscule), so don't be misled by size, or by architectural beauties. Is it suitable for the species of animal? Is there furniture in the cage – branches, logs, swings, barrels, etc.? Can the animals get to a place secluded from the public? Can they get away from each other?

(*Remember, when you are being harsh, that a lot of zoos, through lack of money, are using cages dating back to Victorian times. At the same time, be sure to notice that many zoos are creating new cages which are worse than the Victorian ones.*)

Look for the water supply. Is it clean and plentiful?

(*Please remember that some animals use their dishes, ponds or lakes as lavatories, which makes life difficult. Others wash their food in it, or bathe in it. However, diligent inspection can tell the difference between dirty, fresh water and dirty, five-day-old water.*)

Look for cleanliness. I do not mean if a cage has obviously not been cleaned out that day. Does it look as though it was ever cleaned out thoroughly?

(*Your living-room at the end of the day shows signs that you have lived in it, but it is basically clean; thus a cage should give the appearance of being cared for, but lived in. It should not look as if it was given a lick and a promise during the American revolution.*)

Now we come to what to ask. Those of you who are students of human nature and the depths of prevarication to which homo sapiens can sink, may get a lot of fun out of this.

First, ask what purpose does this collection of animals fulfil.

(*It could be scientific, conservation, educational or amusement. It should, of course, be all four, but it is generally only the latter.*)

Ask if they study their animals. If so, do they publish their findings? If so, where? Ask if they have a filing system and how complex it is. Ask what they have bred, when they bred it, how many they breed a year and have they bred them to the second, third, or fourth generation. Do they publish this information? Where?

(*A very good and wise zoo director once said to me; 'Any fool, with luck, can breed an animal once. You can only say you are successful when you are breeding them regularly and to the second and third generation.'*)

If there are single animals in the collection, ask why they do not have mates. Ask also whether they are prepared to lend *their* single specimens to other zoos for breeding purposes.

Ask what their death rate is per annum. Do they keep it on file, and do they publish it? Are the animals that die sent for post-mortem?

What is the administrator's overall attitude to the conservation of animal life and what are they doing to assist it?

What threatened species are they breeding? Have they got them in pairs, or colonies?

(*It is scarcely any use talking about your great contribution to conservation if you simply have a pair of animals that breed once a year and of whose progeny you immediately dispose.*)

What success are they having in breeding endangered species?

How self-supporting are they in terms of breeding their own animals, both rare and common?

(*The ultimate aim of any responsible zoo should be to reach a point where they are entirely self-sufficient in their breeding and do not have to act as a further drain upon wild stocks.*)

What are their future plans for conservation?
What are their future plans for education?
What are their future plans for the scientific investigation of the species they keep?
What research work is planned?

I am not suggesting that every zoo should be able to give you an adequate reply to each of these questions, nor necessarily measure up to the standards that I have suggested you look for. What I *am* suggesting is that every zoo should be asked these questions with increasing frequency and belligerence, so that they are eventually forced out of their lethargy into improving their standards and thinking seriously about what their role is supposed to be.

But to return to us. What we have tried to do in Jersey is to create a new sort of zoo. I think we have succeeded. We have made many mistakes and will probably make many more, but we are still in our infancy. Before I started in Jersey, I was told a great many things by a great number of people and all these predictions have proved wrong.

I was told that I would never gain support in such a remote place as Jersey. At the time of writing, we have over 15,000 members spread around the world from Peking to Pretoria, from Sydney to Seattle. We are visited by over 200,000 visitors a year and this figure grows annually.

I was told that the inherent difficulties of keeping and breeding rare and threatened animals were enormous, insurmountable in many cases. Though I am not suggesting that breeding wild animals is a simple operation, it can be done, as is proved by our breeding record which, for our size, is phenomenal and improving yearly.

I was told you could not keep large quantities of the same species of animal on display, or the public would get bored. One of our major exhibits consists of six aviaries containing nothing but White-eared pheasants. There is a large explanatory notice, outlining our success with these birds and the reason for our work with them. We have found that the public are fascinated by the story and applaud our efforts. No one has displayed any signs of ennui.

I was told I would never get people with university degrees to undertake the 'menial' tasks of looking after the animals. I said I did not believe it; to be qualified did not mean deified. Fifty per cent of our staff is qualified, happily doing 'menial' work, because of the close contact they thus obtain with the animals and the studies this allows them to undertake and to publish in our Annual Report and other scientific publications.

Last, and probably most important, I was told that my ideas of captive breeding to assist in saving species threatened with extinction were, variously, futile, or cruel, or biologically unsound. Today, what I have been advocating from the age of sixteen, is coming into being : captive breeding groups are being set up throughout the world. They are not always in the best of hands, but never mind, it is a start. Even that massive and most conservative of bodies, the International Union for the Conservation of Nature, is admitting, with a certain Teutonic caution, that captive breeding may well help to save certain species.

In our next step, we plan to form the Trust into a kind of mini-university of wildlife husbandry and breeding. I must stress that this would not be a keeper-training programme, such as some zoological gardens are putting into operation. These are excellent and much needed, but this would be something quite different and much more detailed and comprehensive and would not, of course, concern itself simply with zoological gardens and their maintenance.

If I may criticize the conservation scene (with particular reference to controlled breeding programmes) I would point out the strange and quite unnecessary gulf that seems to exist between the so-called practical and the scientifically qualified man. This gulf is a wide one and can be damaging. The fault lies on both sides : the practical man tends to shy away from the qualified man, trailing what looks like an entire alphabet after his name; the qualified man, on the other hand, tends to believe the practical man, without qualifications, is a mumbling illiterate.

As usual, the truth lies mid-way between the two extremes. I know practical men that I would not put in charge of a dead chihuahua and qualified men who, coming from the rarified heights of science, cannot recognize an animal as being one unless it is floating, immobile, in a tank of formaldehyde. I know some most knowledgeable practical men who can only communicate their valuable experience in a series

153

of inarticulate grunts and I also know qualified men who can only impart their valuable information in a tangled series of twelve-syllable words. Between the Neanderthal grunt and the polysyllabic fluting we must find common ground. This mutual suspicion between the qualified and the practical man leads to a lack of liaison, which, as I say, can be very damaging in the field of controlled breeding.

Examples of what I mean can be found dotted throughout the various volumes of the *Red Data Books,* published by the International Union for the Conservation of Nature. These excellent publications, a list of the endangered mammals, birds and reptiles of the world, together with information about their past and present distribution, contain sections which deal with the number of that particular species held in captivity and their possible breeding potential in captivity. In many cases, the section headed breeding potential is left blank, which is a correct and scientific confession of ignorance, but in a number of cases there are written the words, 'unknown, probably nil' or 'unknown, probably poor'. A good example is the sub-species of the Serval, *Felis serval constantina.* Under the breeding potential in captivity the entry reads, 'the Serval appears not to produce very well in captivity and I have found two records'. The fact is that quite a number of zoological collections have bred Servals and we, to date, have recorded 35 births – one specimen has had thirteen sets of cubs, twenty-nine cubs in all.

This misinformation is due to the qualified not seeking the advice of the practical. Diligent research will uncover many examples of the reverse situation as well. This is only one aspect of it. Another and equally alarming one is that, as controlled breeding programmes become more fashionable among conservationists, more and more heavily qualified people are going to be put in charge of them, and these are generally the people with no practical experience.

Everyone seems hypnotized by university degrees. They are, of course, useful, but if the person concerned is to involve himself or herself with a captive breeding programme, they must have the added qualifications of being able to shovel manure, carry a bucket of water or a bale of hay, get dirty and tired and get to know the living animal, as opposed to the textbook one : they can be very different. As I say, fifty per cent of our staff is qualified, but they do this hard work of looking after the animals, as well as studying them.

In the future the idea is that this Trust should enlarge the range of its breeding specimens (remembering always our limitations of size), for there are many groups which we do not have represented in the collection yet which fall within the scope of our work. For example, we have none of the Edentata (anteaters, armadillos, etc.), nor do we have any of the Canidae (dogs, foxes and so on). Thus we hope to add to the collection viable breeding groups of some of the endangered members of such groups. Once this is done, the collection will be extremely comprehensive and serve a dual purpose; the breeding groups would be of endangered species that urgently need controlled breeding programmes to help them, and they would also be acting as a teaching tool. Already, with grants from our United States sister organization, we have set up a nutritional research laboratory which, we hope, will give us invaluable information in the future and, with another most generous grant, we are in the process of building a veterinary hospital and research unit with X-ray and post-mortem facilities and a well-equipped recovery room for those creatures undergoing extensive treatment.

For this teaching scheme we will need further laboratories in which both students and visiting scientists may study and accommodation in which they can live, a lecture hall, and a small still and cinematographic studio and recording laboratory. When this is all completed – and it is only lack of funds that prevents us doing it immediately – the Trust's headquarters will be, in effect, a complex conservation laboratory in which not only will breeding colonies of threatened species be established, but every aspect of these creatures, biologically, will be studied and finally, most important of all, qualified personnel can be trained to undertake captive breeding programmes anywhere in the world that they are needed.

Selected students could come to the Trust headquarters to undergo an intensive controlled breeding training course. First, by working in every section-in the collection, they would get an excellent overall training in the varied techniques of breeding with a wide range of species – mammals, birds and reptiles. They could then go on to specialize in the creatures emanating from their particular part of the world. At intervals, they would have both oral and written examinations, the students could return home and, with the constant help and advice of this Trust and its staff, be in a position to assist their governments, or the conservation organizations, to form breeding centres in places where such projects should be established.

This would not be simple zoo-keeping but teaching the techniques of animal husbandry of the type in which we specialize : the techniques of building up viable self-sustaining breeding groups of a species with a view, ultimately, to returning specimens from these groups to the wild so as to repopulate areas or revitalize anaemic wild populations. Such work requires the student to be hard-working, meticulous and, above all, dedicated. It is to be hoped that these students would be funded by grants from their governments or by conservation organizations. Thus the Trust would become something that is most urgently needed, a form of university for the teaching of controlled breeding techniques, where people can get the correct training in animal husbandry and then take their talents back to form conservation units throughout the world.

This is what we plan to do. I and the people who work with me think the task is urgent, important and, above all, constructive. We hope, now that you have finished this book, that you will think the same. If so, will you help us by becoming a member of the Trust? Our annual fees are small and we try to keep them that way, acting on the principle that 15,000 members paying modest fees put an organization into a stronger position than 5,000 paying a lot. Unlike most charities, you can come and see what your money is being spent on and it gives us and the animals great pleasure to meet you. So, on behalf of the multitude of charming and bizarre, colourful and exotic, fascinating, resourceful, magnificent, dignified, funny and beguiling minority in this world (who cannot read, write, vote or invent nerve gas) I invite you to join us. Please write to me for details at :

The Wildlife Preservation Trust International,

Les Augres Manor,

Trinity,

Jersey,

Channel Islands.

The Nocturnal House